I0480390

ART BOOKS

FROM CRESCENT MOON PUBLISHING

Leonardo da Vinci
by James Pearson

Early Netherlandish Painting
by Rosalind Mutter

Piero della Francesca
by Naomi Haskell

Giovanni Bellini
by Julia Davis

Eric Gill: Nuptials of God
by Anthony Hoyland

Minimal Art and Artists In the 1960s and After
by Laura Garrard

Postwar Art
by George Knighton

Vincent van Gogh: Visionary Landscapes
by Stuart Morris

Max Beckmann
by Stuart Morris

Egon Schiele: Sex and Death in Purple Stockings
by D. Simon Eade

Mark Rothko: The Art of Transcendence
by Julia Davis

Jasper Johns
by L.M. Poole

Brice Marden
by Laura Garrard

Frank Stella: American Abstract Artist
by James Pearson

FRA ANGELICO

FRA ANGELICO

A SKETCH

JENNIE ELLIS KEYSOR

Author of "Sketches of American Authors"

"Art manifests whatever is most exalted, and it manifests it to all"

– TAINE

CRESCENT MOON

First published 1900. This edition © 2017.

Printed and bound in the U.S.A.
Set in Book Antiqua 10 on 14pt.
Designed by Radiance Graphics.

British Library Cataloguing in Publication data

ISBN-13 9781861716033

CRESCENT MOON PUBLISHING
P.O. Box 1312, Maidstone, Kent, ME14 5XU
Great Britain, www.crmoon.com

CONTENTS

NOTE ON THE TEXT

The text is from *Fra Angelico* by Jennie Keysor published by Education Company, Boston, 1900.

The illustrations in the text are included in the illustrations section, along with many other works.

"The art of Angelico, both as a colorist and a draughtsman, is consummate; so perfect and so beautiful that his work may be recognized at a distance by the rainbow-play and brilliancy of it: however closely it may be surrounded by other works of the same school, glowing with enamel and gold, Angelico's may be told from them at a glance, like so many huge pieces of opal among common marbles."

– JOHN RUSKIN.

"The light of his studio came from Paradise."

– PAUL DE ST. VICTOR.

"His world is a strange one – a world not of hills and fields and flowers and men of flesh and blood, but one where the people are embodied ecstasies, the colors tints from evening clouds or apocalyptic jewels, the scenery a flood of light or a background of illuminated gold. His mystic gardens, where the ransomed souls embrace and dance with angels on the lawns outside the City of the Lamb, are such as were never trodden by the foot of man in any paradise of earth." "Fra Angelico's Madonnas are beings of unearthly beauty, and words fail to convey any idea of their ineffable loveliness and purity. His angels too are creatures of another sphere, and purer types have never yet been conceived in art. The drawing of the hands of his angels and Madonnas is most exquisite – charming in tender yet subtle simplicity of outline."

– TIMOTHY COLE.

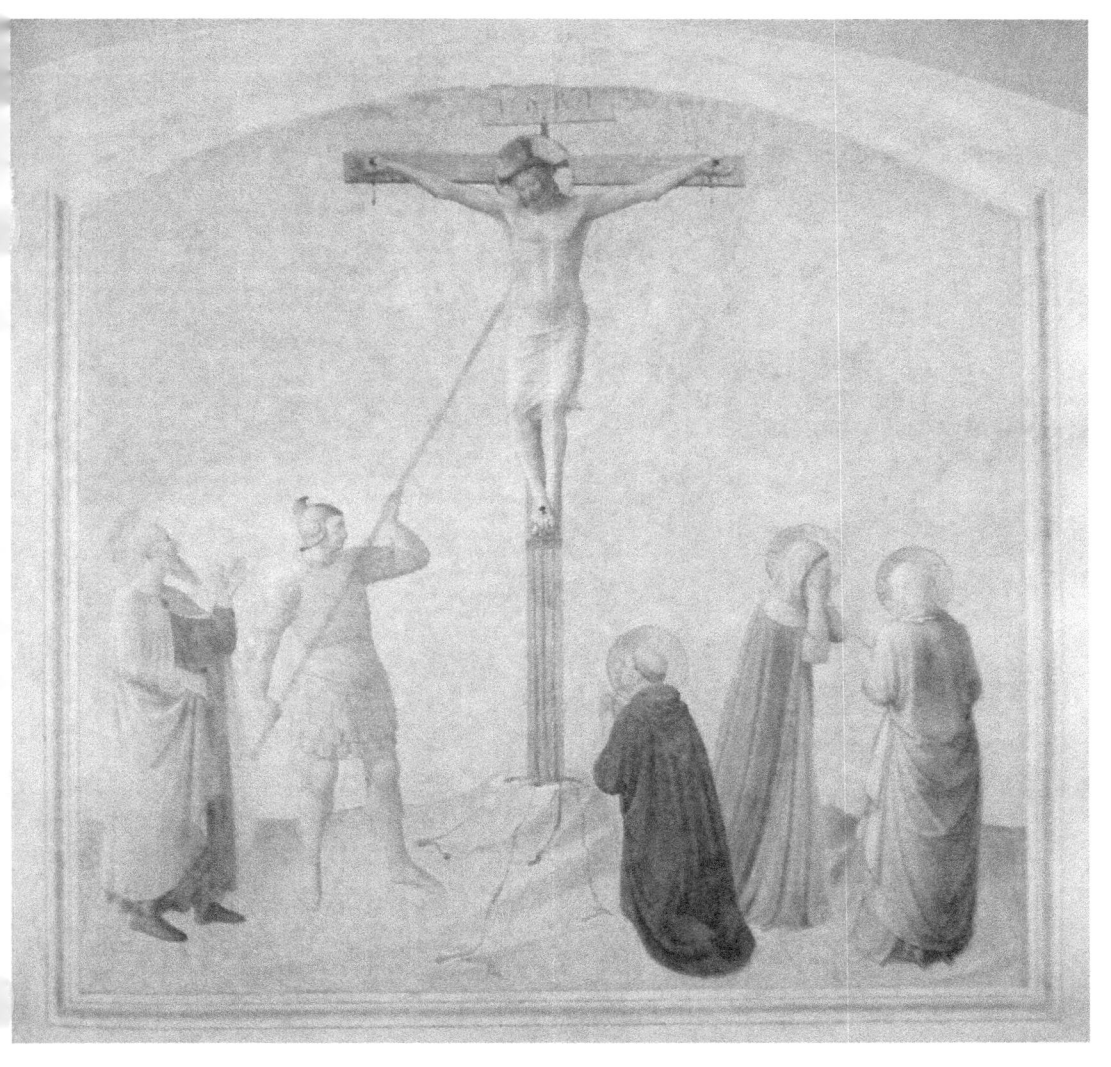

Fra Angelico, Crucifixion, cell 42, San Marco

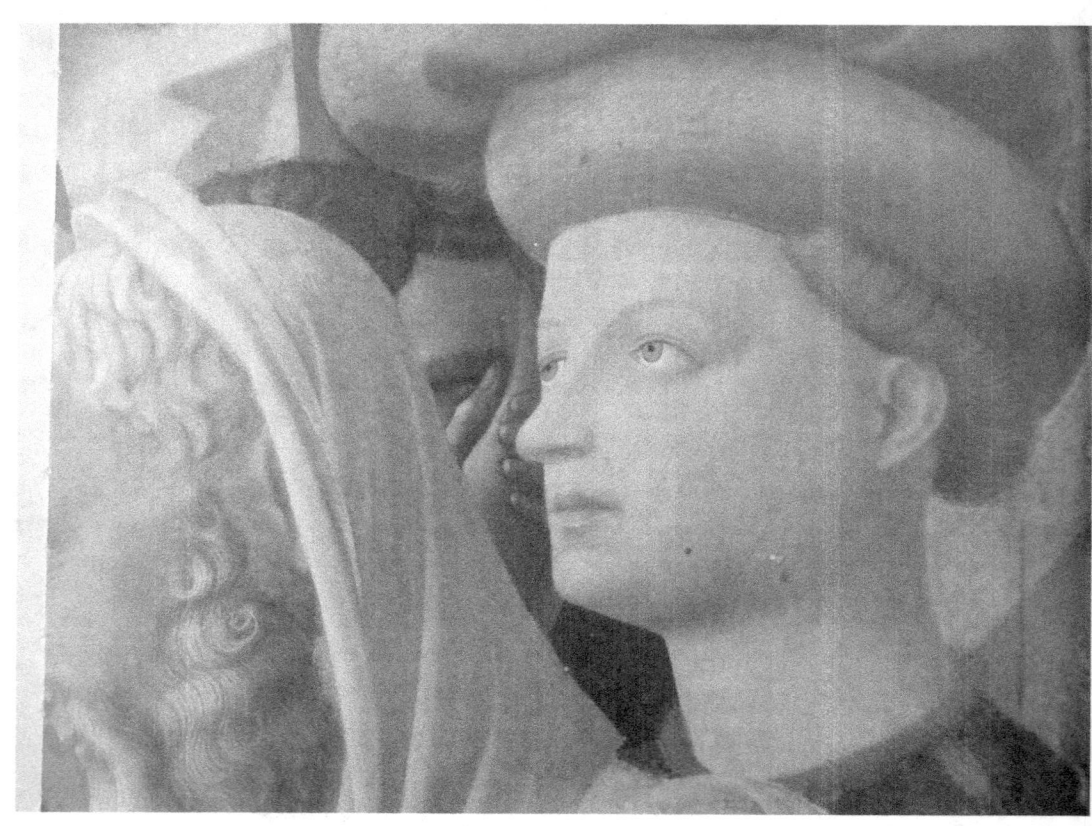

Fra Angelico, Descent From the Cross, detail, San Marco

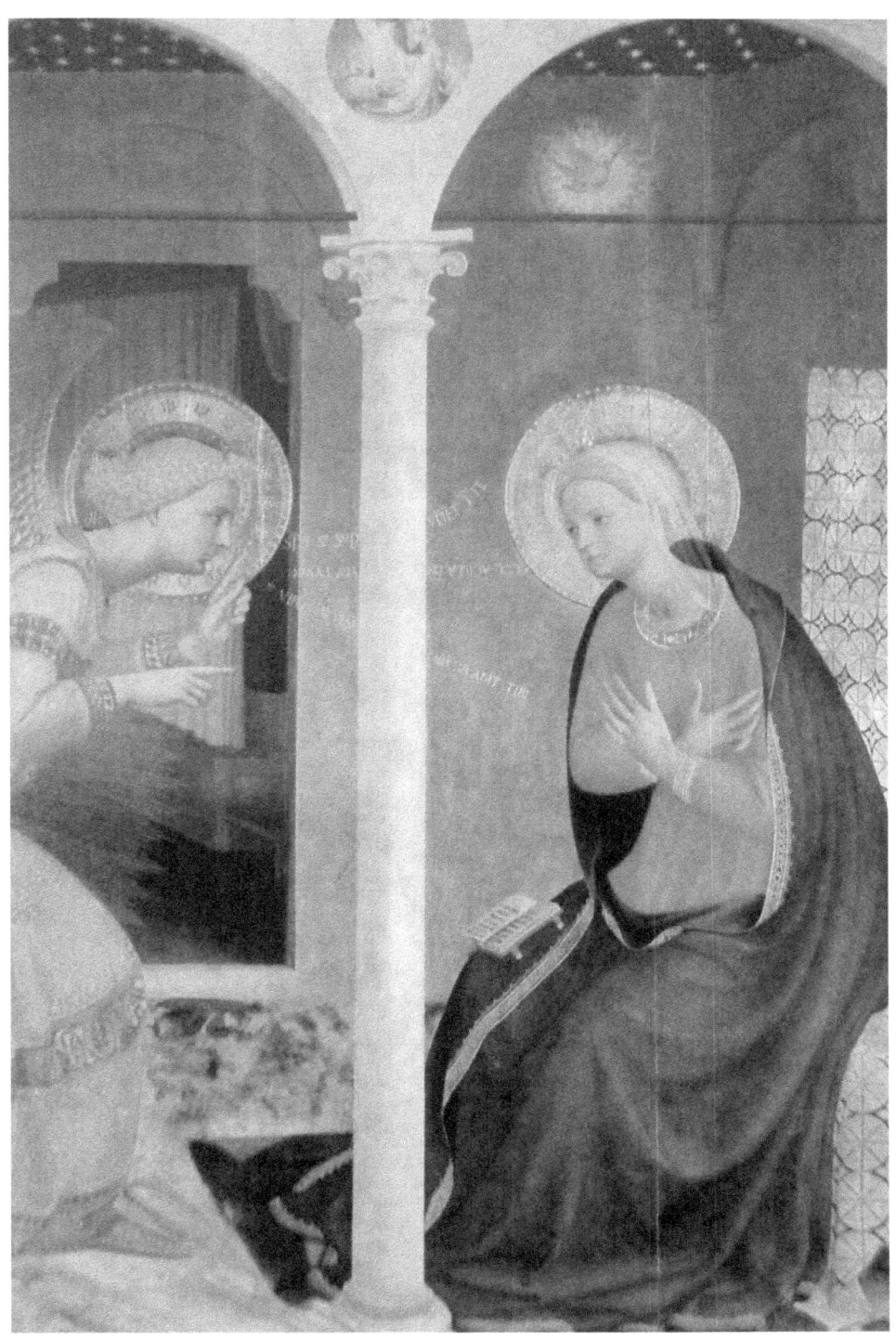

Fra Angelico, Anunciation, Cortona

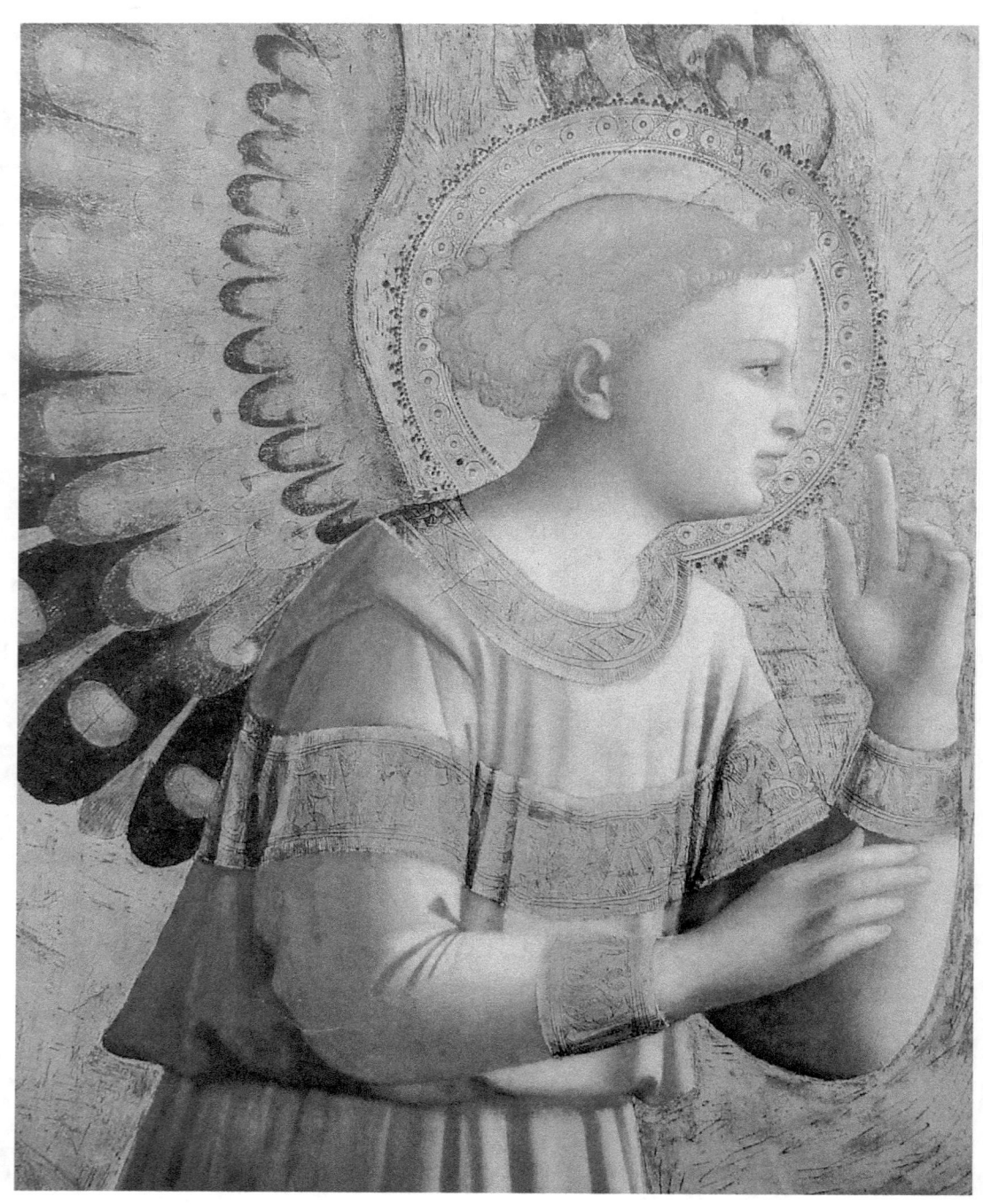

Fra Angelico, Annunciatory Angel, c. 1437-46, Detroit Institute of Arts

FRA ANGELICO

1387 – 1455

Let us for a few moments turn our attention to a monastery a short distance from Florence. From its elevated position on the hills which skirt the vale of the Arno it commands a panoramic view of the "Lily City." It is the time when the Renaissance is virgin new to the world. Faith was still so real and living a thing that men and women shut themselves up from the world in order to live holy lives and devote themselves entirely to the service of God.

It is a body of such men on the heights of Fiesole that interests us. They are Dominican monks, of the order of great preachers, founded long ago by St. Dominic. Over long white robes the brothers, or frates, as they are called, wear black capes and back from their tonsured heads fall hoods, which protect them in inclement weather. It is a prosperous monastery surrounded by goodly fields. In some, the olive groves blossom in the spring-like snow, or wear foliage of richest green as the season advances. In others, the yellowing grain waves in the upland summer richest green as the season advances. In others, the yellowing grain waves in the upland summer breeze. The monks are busy people, many without in the fields tilling the fruitful soil or gathering in the abundant harvest.

Indoors there is the silence which attends toil, intense and absorbing. The cellar and kitchen are in perfect order and in the refectory, or dining room, the table is spread for the next frugal meal. In the scriptorium, or writing room, several monks are busy copying ancient manuscripts on parchment. One does this work, using the most exquisite lettering, while another indites the hymns long loved by the church. This other, bending over his task, from a rich palette makes the vine to run, the dragon to coil, the angel head to shine, the tropic bird to fly from out the lettering of his book or, more ambitious still, he decorates a broad margin with an elaborate design. Mayhap he devotes an entire page to the deliniation of some favorite saint. –

"What joy it is to labor so,
To see the long-tressed angels grow
Beneath the cunning of his hand,
Vignette and tail-piece subtly wrought!"

Here in the walk of the cloisters, his pallid face lit up by fiery eyes, strolls another, the preacher of the monastery. To-night he will electrify his audience with the eloquence of his sermon that shall tell of the curse of evil, of the saving power of love.

Yonder, with the face and attitude of one who prays, painting a lovely angel with flame upon her forehead, with stars upon her robe and with a golden trumpet in her hand, is a man whose fancy has outgrown the margin, the full page even, of the beloved parchment book, and so he fills a whole wall with his vision from Paradise. Little need is there to name this painter-monk. It is Fra Angelico, the "Angelical Painter," *Il Beato*, "The Blessed."

To this man, who prays as he paints and who paints as he prays, we are to give our attention for a time. It is particularly delightful to find such a character in a time when holy men and women sometimes forgot their religious vows and ordinary citizens, in their scramble for place, lost sight of the laws of honor and manhood. In a time of greed it pleases us to find a man, who, though his art was the fashion of his period, would take no money for his pictures; in a time of ambition for place, to find one who could refuse an elevated position because he did not think himself fitted to fill it; to find a man so simple and yet so wise that he knew the work allotted to him in life and had the devotion to stick to it in spite of inducements to give it up.

Such a man was Fra Angelico, the sweet character, the beautiful artist of heavenly visions, the man to whom Ruskin goes back as the embodiment of correct principles in art, even beyond Raphael, the idol of the ages. Fra Angelico is the last figure of the old simple time in art when the spirit counted for most. He lingered long on the threshold of that later time, when men forgot the spirit in their enthusiasm for copying the real thing as it presents itself in nature.

Now that we know what the prosaic artists of that prosaic time taught, namely to draw correctly, we go back to the visions of the angelical painter and hug them to us as a rich bequest, a glimpse, as it were, of that paradise closed to mortal eyes. Along other lines too, it is good for us to study the men and women who were great enough to be simple, to be devoted. In art it is quite as good and equally delightful.

Whoever tells the story of Fra Angelico's life has few dates and events with which to entangle his reader's treacherous memory. The story is told when the man and his spirit have been portrayed, when his surroundings at various periods have been described. It is forced home to us, therefore, that we ought to know well the history of the company of men to whom he belonged and was devotedly attached for almost fifty years of his life.

We have already spoken of these monks at Fiesole and of their pursuits. As they gazed out upon Florence, the matchless city of the Arno, it was with longing hearts as homesick children, for they had been banished from the loved city as a matter of discipline, years before. As they looked out from their commanding windows, they forgot the glorious scenery about them in an intense desire to be at home again. In a small way they shared the agonized grief of Dante, an exile in Ravenna's drear waters, when he knocked in vain at the closed gates of his loved and native Florence. Theirs, however, was a kinder fate than that which befell the renowned poet, for they were recalled to Florence.

The monastery of San Marco was emptied of some monks of another order and the place given over to the reformed Dominicans. Singing hymns of praise, arrayed in their black and white, they filed down from the heights of Fiesole to San Marco, while the expelled monks departed with downcast mien and sore lamentations.

The restored monks found San Marco hardly fit for habitation, so ruinous was its condition. Cosimo de Medici came to their relief and repaired and beautified the building. In addition, he had a sort of chapel or retiring room fitted up in it for himself to which he might come for quiet and for consultation. Willingly the monks dwelt in huts while the repairs and decorations were going forward. We shall learn later how Angelico embellished the walls of cloister and cell until the thoughts of the angelical brother were laid bare to his companions, so that, to-day, perhaps the chief reason for the throng of visitors to this unattractive building is the fact that here Fra Angelico lived and painted.

The Dominicans were restored to Florence and their home, San Marco, began its career, if, indeed, we may say that a building can have a career, as an essential factor in Florentine history.

We may love Fra Angelico but, after all, the most interesting association in many minds for San Marco is not his sweet life in its brotherhood or his heavenly faces upon its walls, but rather that here studied, taught, preached and died Savonarola, that pure patriot, that noble, although often mistaken man, that most eloquent orator that Florence has given to the world. As simple as Angelico and as free from place-seeking, he was the soul and voice of the Florentine people when faction rent the city and threatened its very existence. That clear voice, prompted by a magnificent love, by a burning zeal, sometimes makes us forget that the zeal was often misguided, and that disobedience to authority is not always the best way of effecting reform.

San Marco, standing off there from the Duomo, is a plain building, but to the thoughtful visitor to-day there are echoes of footfalls sounding down those tenantless halls, which make the heart quicken its beating, the cheek flush, and the eye dim; for it is Savonarola's voice that he hears, Angelico's brush that he marks, the wise counsel of Antonio that falls on his ear, instead of the sights and sounds of sense.

Three times, at least, in the history of Italian art a pure light, a fresh stream has flowed in from the hills – Raphael from Urbino among the heights of Umbria, Titian from the crags of Cadore and now Angelico from the slopes of the Apennines in the fertile district of Mugello. Each brought with him from his native hills a vigor and devotion new to the dwellers below.

At Vecchio, a small town crowning one of the spurs of the Apennines, Fra Angelico was born, in 1387. His father was a certain Pietro, or Peter, and there was an older son who afterwards bore the name Benedetto. Now, the name *Angelico,* by which we love to call our angel painter, was really not his name at all. He was simply Guido, the son of Pietro, and when he entered the monastery he was given yet another name, Giovanni, or John. Fate, or fame rather, destined that he should not be known either by his birth name or by his religious name. What his hand could do, what his heart could show were the things which determined his name. Because he painted angels so matchlessly they called him Brother or Fra Angelico, because his heart opened so unselfishly to his fellow men they called him *Beato,* "The Blessed," and by these names we know him to-day.

From what Vasari tells us, that Guido might have lived at ease had he so desired, we know that his father was a man of means. What the boy's education was we are unable to tell definitely. From the surroundings of his home at Vecchio we can infer much, especially in the light of Angelico's later work. Hardly twenty miles from Florence, on the road to Ravenna, the hill town of Vecchio must have taken a keen interest in the stirring events ever going on in the Florence of the early Renaissance.

We can imagine, however, that, though these things impressed the young Guido, the beautiful scenery surrounding his home held a deeper meaning for him. Here were fine olive groves, there rocks grew bare and jagged, refusing to produce anything except scrubby underbrush. A frowning precipice yonder lost none of its forbidding character because of the crown it wore – a fine castle, which told by its towers and turrets, where watchmen stood or paced throughout the lonely hours, that the age when lusty knights rode forth to harry each other's domain was not wholly past.

That castle, gleaming white and menacing through the olive trees, is one of the country seats of the powerful Medicean family. The boy Guido and his brother have often seen the great Cosimo walking in his garden or riding on the highway. Indeed, the boys have been accosted by him and questioned regarding their sports.

It was not, however, the power of man, who plants his dwellings on the heights of the earth or grows fat upon the produce of her soil, that most deeply impressed our young artist. To him the pearly white of the summer cloud, the cerulean blue of the endless depths of air, the amethyst, ruby and topaz of the sky at sunrise or sunset were more. They seemed but reflections of a glory beyond cloud and sky, where the hosts of the blessed forever praise their redeeming Lord. Those soft and melting colors slid into his soul and years later he poured them forth in the garment of some trumpeting angel, blessed Madonna, or rejoicing brother.

In his tenderness for nature we can imagine that the little creatures of the woods fled not at his approach but rather stayed to receive from his hand food or a loving caress. The flowers that bespangled the soft Tuscan turf sprung up after his foot had pressed them, so light was his step, so gentle the thought that in him reigned. The boys were constantly together, sharing in the rambles and sports which their home region encouraged. Their love increased until it was sealed by the vow that made them brother monks as well as brothers in flesh and blood.

At the age of fourteen Guido left home, probably for purposes of study, but we cannot trace his course during purposes of study, but we cannot trace his course during the next six years. We know not if, like Titian, he crushed flowers to obtain their colors to paint with, in his boyhood days, but somehow, somewhere in those early years he learned the rudiments of the art by which the world knows him to-day.

With such a boyhood, remote from the marts of trade, surrounded by all that is loveliest in nature, we are not surprised to find him at the age of twenty anxious to follow a religious life. It is possible that, during those six years just previous to his entering the convent, he may have studied miniature painting or illuminating in some monastery, where his purpose to become a monk took definite form. However that may be, in 1407, he sought out the monastery of Fiesole and entered as a novice, to begin the study and privations which should prepare him for the life of a Dominican friar. To his great joy his elder brother joined him soon after and was given the name Benedetto.

The novices were sent for a time to the older convent of Cortona. Here the training in the love of Nature, which began in the hills of Vecchio, was continued. The convent of Cortona stood upon an elevation overlooking the placid waters of Lake Trasemene, where, in ancient times, Hannibal gained a great victory over the Romans. All about were the remains of massive masonry, built in the remote past by the Etruscans. Three islands broke the quiet surface of the little lake and on one of them stood a monastery. I wonder if, on days of relaxation, the holy men, rowing across to visit their brothers of the island, did not catch some of the finny tribe that inhabited the lake, or snare some of the wild fowl that lived along its margin.

Our angelical painter probably was not attracted by such matters. The prospect of lake and hill and wood, which daily opened before him, deepened all his early impressions and so, almost unconsciously, the training for his future and so, almost unconsciously, the training for his future work continued. Meanwhile, too, he probably practiced assiduously in the parchment books of the monastery the art of illumination.

Shortly after Angelico took upon himself the full vows of a monk, the whole religious body of Fiesole was removed to Foligno. Here they remained for several years, until the plague broke out and they fled to Cortona, the same town where Angelico had spent several years of his novitiate. By this time he had become a full fledged painter, as is shown by the work he left in two Dominican churches of Cortona. There is reason to believe that when Angelico, an old man, was on his way to Rome to paint for the Pope, he gave, in exchange for the courtesies of the convent of Cortona to a traveller, some pictures of the Madonna which are still to be seen in the church of St. Dominic in Cortona.

The brotherhood was later recalled to Fiesole. Angelico must often have gone down to Florence and there have seen the work of his great contemporaries in art. Massaccio was the artist, above all others, who was attracting attention at this time. His work was the most accurate representation of real things that had yet been made by any artist in Italy. Fra Angelico must have seen his work and profited by it, too.

But he never forgot his early inspiration drawn from the hills and from the morning and evening skies, and so he went back, in spite of any small influence of the new art, to pore over the parchment page and to make the vision of his soul write itself down in fadeless color on golden backgrounds. What he saw of artists' work outside of the convent had one marked influence, however. Our devout painter began to feel trammeled by the narrowness of a margin, indeed of an entire page, and he turned to the ample space furnished by the walls of convent and church. the walls of convent and church.

It was shortly after the return of the brotherhood from Cortona that they were given the church and convent of San Marco in Florence. After long absence they were to return home and their hearts were lifted in song. When the repairs were completed, Cosimo bethought him of the painter-monk of the brotherhood, and asked him to make the house beautiful for his brethren. Whether Cosimo remembered those early days when he had accosted two boys in the vicinity of his castle we do not know, but it seems certain that he knew of the mature artist's work and his reputation throughout Tuscany.

It must have been a great joy to Fra Giovanni to be given this congenial task in which he could glorify God and gratify his own passion for art. Henceforth he left the parchment books to his brother to embellish while he occupied himself on the larger space his soul had long craved.

Lest this work, which he loved so dearly, should be done in a spirit of self-indulgence, he laid certain strictures upon himself in carrying it on. He believed that he had a message direct from God to bear to men through his pictures, so he never undertook one of them without prefacing the work with a season of fasting and prayer, and then, when he began his work, he never changed a stroke lest he prove disobedient to the heavenly vision. Often and often his lips moved in prayer while his hand laid on the colors of the robes or the gold of the background.

While he painted the Crucifixion tears streamed down his cheeks in sympathy with the agony there endured. The pictures of a man who painted in such a spirit are not mere works of art. They are more, for they lay bare to us a human soul, making the thoughts he thought our own, the devoutness and sympathy he felt a part of our own lives.

Savonarola thundered forth his message from the pulpit of San Marco; Angelico delivered his, more enduring, though hardly less eloquent, on his knees, through the rainbow colors on his palette. In an age when monasteries and convents were an essential part of civilization, it was a mighty contribution that San

Marco gave to the world in the earnest preacher, in the angelic painter. Both were simple men, great in their devotion, leaders of their age in their respective places, but the one was wending along a quiet way that should terminate peacefully in a secluded grave in Rome, while the other was moving on like a whirlwind, tearing up many things sacred in its course and ending in a violent death.

Everyone talks of Angelico's work in San Marco. Let us see what it was, what we should look for were we to go there to-day. In the cloister, where the monks were constantly passing to and fro, are many of his best works. Here above a doorway, is "*St. Peter, Martyr*" standing with his finger on his lips in token of the silence that should reign in a holy house. Above another door two of the brotherhood welcome their Lord, a weary traveller.

In a larger space he has painted the angel Gabriel announcing the coming of the Christ Child to the youthful Mary. The sweet submissiveness of Mary together with her mild surprise at the angelic appearance, the grace and earnestness of Gabriel, with his wings still spread, as if just alighted from heaven, are wholly to our satisfaction for representing this naive scene from sacred history.

Here, too, we find the solemn last scene in the Christ-drama, as "*The Annunciation*" was the first. "*The Crucifixion*," which we find here, was simply portrayed, but with a pathos that Angelico's sympathetic nature would naturally show. It was afterwards reproduced in each of the cells.

In the chapter house we find a more elaborate representation of the Crucifixion. Here it is large enough to fill an entire wall and its excellence hardly in proportion to its size. The attention is drawn from the great central figure to the figures at the foot of the Cross, whose awe and adoration are well expressed by the painter. It was in the room adorned-with this great fresco, that George Eliot had Romola and Savonarola meet in their famous interview. That the presence of the solemn picture added force to that powerful scene goes without saying.

Into the cloisters, the chapter house, the chapel, men of the world might enter and look about. Not so the narrow cells, huddled together, where each monk was supposed to commune with his Lord in uninterrupted silence. For these narrow cells, forty in number, Fra Angelico did his best work, believing, doubtless, with the ancient builders that "The gods see everywhere." The subjects selected were the events in Christ's life and to each cell was given one chapter, as it subjects selected were the events in Christ's life and to each cell was given one chapter, as it were, from the wondrous story. Nothing could more forcibly prove the absolute devotion of the painter, his total disregard for the attention of men, than his dedication of his best work to the narrow and dimly lighted cells of San Marco.

Long ago the good brothers of San Marco were sent away and the doors thrown wide to the public, who now call it the Museum of San Marco. Easel pictures have been gathered here to swell the number of Angelico's works in the place that was so long his home. One of these is a small copy, made by the artist, of what is known to us as the "*Tabernacle Madonna*" which is in the Uffizi gallery in Florence. The glory of this work is not in the Madonna or the child she holds but, strange to say, in the frame which encloses the picture. A broad band of smooth gold intervenes between the outer and inner molding of the frame and in this space are painted the twelve angels playing various musical instruments, which are so familiar to us to-day.

Since Angelico's time, no matter what artist has essayed the task of angel painting, none has approached so nearly as the angelical painter of San Marco to our ideal of these heavenly beings. We all of us have some more or less definite notions of how angels should look. We may be painfully literal on other subjects but, though there is no science on which to base our demand, we want them with white or jeweled wings. Sometimes, in our most rapt moods, the air about us seems filled with these ethereal beings, tending on the sick and dying, leading little children, ministering to prisoners as to Peter of old, bringing comfort to us in our sorrows. This, of course, is a fancy and yet it is such fancies that have made Fra Angelico's representations of angels a real joy to man through all the centuries since he painted them with more than mortal power.

His angels that we enjoy most are not those entrusted with some special mission, but they are of that great multitude whose joy it is to bring good tidings of great joy to men. Here is one glowing in ruby red, the color of passion. She lifts on high her golden trumpet and we know that God is a ready helper, waiting only to be summoned to our rescue. Another, arrayed all in green, the color of spring, brings us hope, without which man would be crushed by the iron weight of his sorrows. This one in blue bears her message of heavenly love and fidelity. That one in yellow, the color of the sun itself, brings light to those who sit in darkness. Truly they are a ministering band with their halo-encircled heads, their heavenward-lifted eyes, their star-bespangled robes.

What matter if critics tell us that Angelico's knowledge of anatomy was defective and that it is fortunate for his angels that their creator represented them all closely draped? Their talk for centuries has not made the devout painter's fame one whit less, while all the time his angels have been bringing comfort to generations of men and women.

Another picture in San Marco we scan carefully. It is "*The Coronation of the Virgin.*" This was a favorite subject with the painter, perhaps because it represents the final reward of the world's great mother – the crown placed upon her head by her enthroned Son. We remember how exquisitely Correggio depicted the same event, with what supreme grace his lovely virgin bends her matchless head to receive the diadem. Hardly less beautiful are Fra Angelico's pictures of this subject, even though they were painted half a century before Correggio's birth. The best of subject, even though they were painted half a century before Correggio's birth. The best of Angelico's pictures of "*The Coronation of the Virgin*" is now in the Louvre, where the beautiful

Virgin is surrounded by tier upon tier of rejoicing angels.

For nearly forty years Fra Angelico had served his convent faithfully, with devout life and the work of his hand. Everything paid for his pictures went to swell the income of the convent. He never took an order without first consulting his prior.

His fame had long ago reached Rome. The art-loving Popes of that time could not remain oblivious to his great ability. In 1445, the quiet life of the monastery was interrupted by Pope Eugenius, who called Angelico to Rome to assist in decorating the Vatican. We can easily imagine that there was some shrinking on Angelico's part at severing the ties that had held him so long among the brothers of his order. This may have been somewhat offset by a vague desire to see Rome, the pilgrim city of the Christian world.

However that may be, he obeyed the call of the Pope and journeyed by easy stages, passing from convent to convent, until the Holy City was reached. It would have been an interesting journey to have taken with the pious monk. One could have seen how the various monasteries exercised one of the most beneficial purposes of their organization, that of ministering to tired and hungry travellers. At many convents at whose doors he appeared, a stranger, he probably left pictures and certainly the memory of a charming personality. Perhaps he relieved for an hour some weary illuminator of the parchment and left a page of his work to encourage the tired monk.

The Pope who called Angelico to Rome did not live long after the painter's arrival there, but he did not die before he had shown special favor to the monk of San Marco.

Taking for granted that, because Angelico could paint such beautiful pictures he could do everything else equally well, he asked him to become the Archbishop of Florence, one of the most important church offices within the gift of the Pope. How we admire the good brother when he responded, with the simplicity which was so marked a characteristic of him, "I can paint pictures but I cannot rule men." And further, how we delight in him as he recommends another brother of his order, Fra Antonio. That his judgement in this matter was equal to his generosity is proved by the fact that Antonio became the wisest archbishop Florence had ever had.

The successor of Pope Eugenius, Nicholas V., also extended his friendship and protection to the painter. Here in Rome he lived for the last ten years of his life. His work here was largely confined to the chapel of Nicholas V., in the Vatican, which he decorated with scenes from the lives of St. Lawrence and St. Stephen. For years this chapel was closed to the public and the key lost, so that when it was re-opened it seemed as if a new set of works belonging to Fra Angelico had been discovered.

When the heat of summer came on in Rome, the painter from the hills of the Arno wilted under the depressing influence and he longed for his native heights. An opportunity for release from the stagnant weather of Rome during the months of June, July and August came from an unexpected quarter. It was the time of the building of the great Italian cathedrals. Every large community seemed bent on excelling its neighbor in the splendor of the church it erected. Florence reared her Duomo, the Santa Maria del Fiore, Siena built her fine cathedral, striped black and yellow like a tiger.

Orvieto, near by, had witnessed a wonderful miracle, and in remembrance of it her citizens determined to build a cathedral that should be more beautiful than any other in Italy. So much in earnest were the people of Orvieto in undertaking this work, that they gave their holidays to drawing materials for it from the hills near by. In eight years, an incredibly short time in the building of a mediaeval cathedral, it was sufficiently finished for holding religious services. It was three hundred years, however, before the people had made it the wrought jewel that it stands to-day.

In the delicacy and elaborateness of its ornament it is the most splendid church in Italy. A hundred and fifty skilled sculptors worked their best on the carving. Nearly a hundred workers in mosaic put together cunningly the bits of glass and precious stones which make its rich and vari-colored mosaic. Almost as many master painters added their work to the precious structure. The facade is like some grand screen, with its exquisite bas-relief, its glistening and intricate mosaic and its delicate pinnacles, every one crowned with a statue.

Such a beautiful and substantial structure was a fine crown for this ancient town, rising almost like a rock-cube from the barren ravines below. It was to help adorn this wonderful church that the building council urged Fra Angelico to quit Rome each year through the sickly summer. All arrangements were completed and our artist once more breathed the hill air to which he was born.

On one of the walls he planned to represent *"The Last Judgment"* a subject which he had previously painted. He never proceeded further than to the completion of the figure of the judging Christ. This fragment is the strongest piece of work Angelico ever did. It is probable that the mighty Angelo studied this figure before painting his own *"Last Judgment."* The critic who compares the two Christs must, it seems to me, ever decide in favor of the one made by the Angelical painter. The combination of strength and compassion in Angelico's is far more to our notions of the gentle Christ, sitting as Judge of all the world. If Angelico had finished the work at Orvieto, it would doubtless have been much like the one we may study to-day in the Academy in Florence. Let us consider that for a moment.

It was a strange subject for one with so mild and loving a nature to undertake, but we must remember that it was the favorite theme of the age, so that all sorts of painters tried their hands at it. Here Christ sits enthroned, encircled by angels, while below him, divided by a long line of unopened graves, are the blessed and the condemned. In depicting the former our angel painter was perfectly at home. What a joyous host they are as they tread the flowery meadows and appear in the searching rays of heaven's own light! One group, a monk embraced by an angel, is reproduced in this sketch.

Even if for a time Angelico was able to summon the power by which he could portray an avenging and yet pitying Christ, he lost that power when he tried to image forth the agony of the condemned, the wickedness of Satan. So the picture stands, half in the glory of fine and characteristic execution and half in the darkness of inadequate workmanship.

Just why Angelico never went back to Orvieto we do not know. It is probable that the infirmities of age were pressing upon him. Perhaps, too, he was reserving his surplus strength for a last visit to his beloved Florence. Hither we know he came, in the last years of his life, and a last visit to his beloved Florence. Hither we know he came, in the last years of his life, and painted for the Church of the Annunciation a little cupboard to hold the gold and silver vessels used about the altar. It was a delicate task not wholly unlike the miniature work with which, in his early years, he had adorned the parchments of his monastery.

Thirty-five panels were filled with scenes from the life of our Lord. The series is done in the spirit of a man who knows the Scriptures and medieval legend to a point, and all the time there shines through the painted figures the saintliness, the mystic, far-away thoughts of the artist. It was a beautiful work to give to his home city in the evening of his quiet life.

The work completed, he wended his way back to Rome where he died, in 1455, or, as a contemporary historian says, "Envious death broke his pencil and his beautiful soul winged its way among the angels to make Paradise more joyous." He was buried in the Church of Santa Maria Sopra Minerva where he had lived since his first coming to Rome. His tomb is simple enough, enriched merely with the quaint figure of a Dominican monk, with his hands crossed, and wearing the dress of his order. At the feet of the stone monk is this epitaph, composed by Nicholas V., Angelico's friend and patron –

"Not that in me a new Apelles lived,
But that thy poor, O Christ, my gains received;

This be my praise: Deeds done for fame on earth
Live not in heaven. Fair Florence gave me birth."

What his appearance was we cannot tell with certainty as no authentic portrait of him remains to us. From imaginary and traditional portraits we get our only notions of how the angelical painter looked, and these are likely to fall far short of giving us correct ideas of the face of one whose character was well-nigh faultless.

Living the secluded life of a monk, we should hardly expect to find many pupils to continue his work after him. One there is, however, who is always spoken of as Angelico's pupil, and that is Benozzo Gozzoli, whose angels at times approach in beauty those of the master-painter of angels. Benozzo was the artist who completed the work that Angelico began at Orvieto.

We have found the facts of Angelico's life few and not at all startling and yet his character was such that it left an indelible impress on his age. We cannot better close this sketch than by quoting from Vasari, who thus sums up the character of his devout countryman:–

"This father, truly angelic, spent all his life in the service of God and for the good of the world and his neighbor. In truth, the great and extraordinary powers possessed by Fra Giovanni could not have existed except in a man of most holy life. He was a man of simplicity and most holy in his ways… He withheld himself from all worldly deeds, and living purely and holily, he was such a friend to the poor that I think his soul is now in heaven.

"He worked continually at his pictures and would never treat any but religious subjects. He might have been a rich man but he cared not to boast, and used to say that true riches consisted in being content with little. He might have had command over many but would not, saying that there was less trouble and risk in obeying than in commanding… He was most gentle and sober, and, living chastely, freed himself from the snares of the world; and he was wont to say that whoever followed art had need of peace and to live without distracting thoughts, and that he who does work that concerns Christ must live continually with Christ.

"He was never known to get angry with the monks; if anyone

desired work from him he would say that he would obtain consent of the Prior to it, and then would not fail to fulfill the request. In fact, this father, who cannot be sufficiently praised, was in all his works and conversation most humble and modest, and in his painting dexterous and conscientious, and the saints of his painting have more the air and resemblance of saints than those of any other painter."

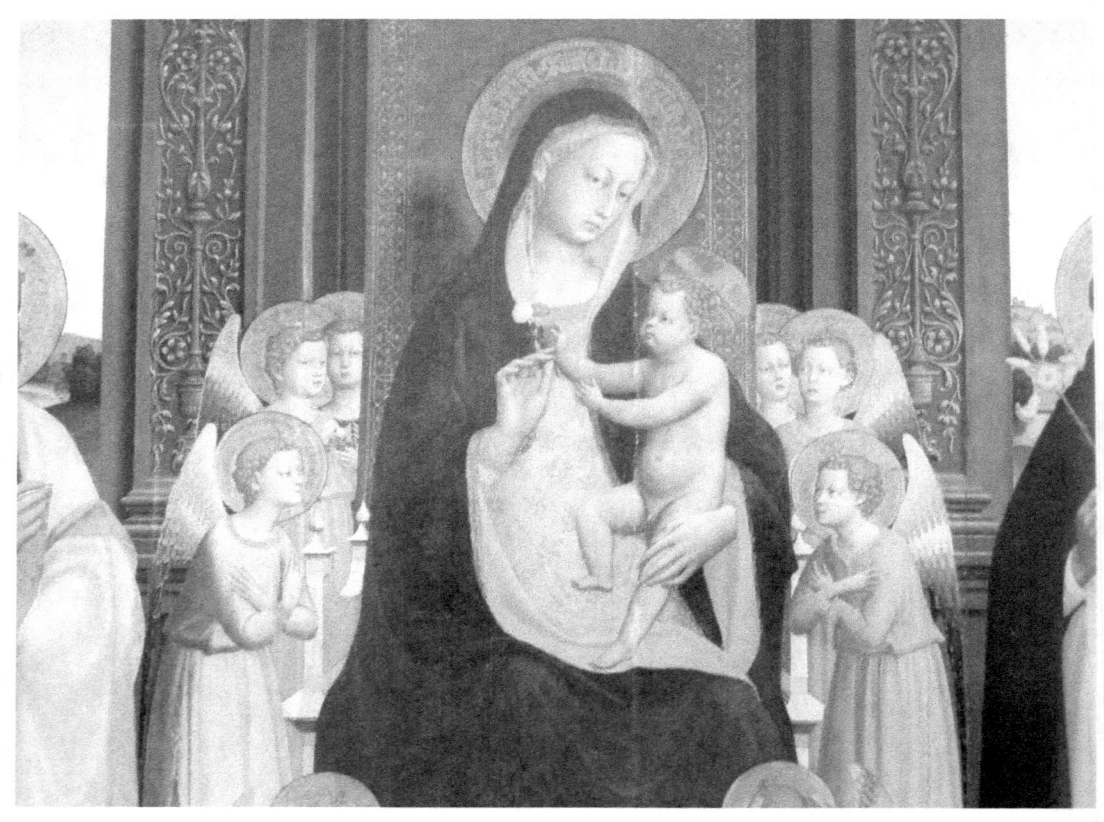

Fra Angelico, Virgin and Child, Fiesole

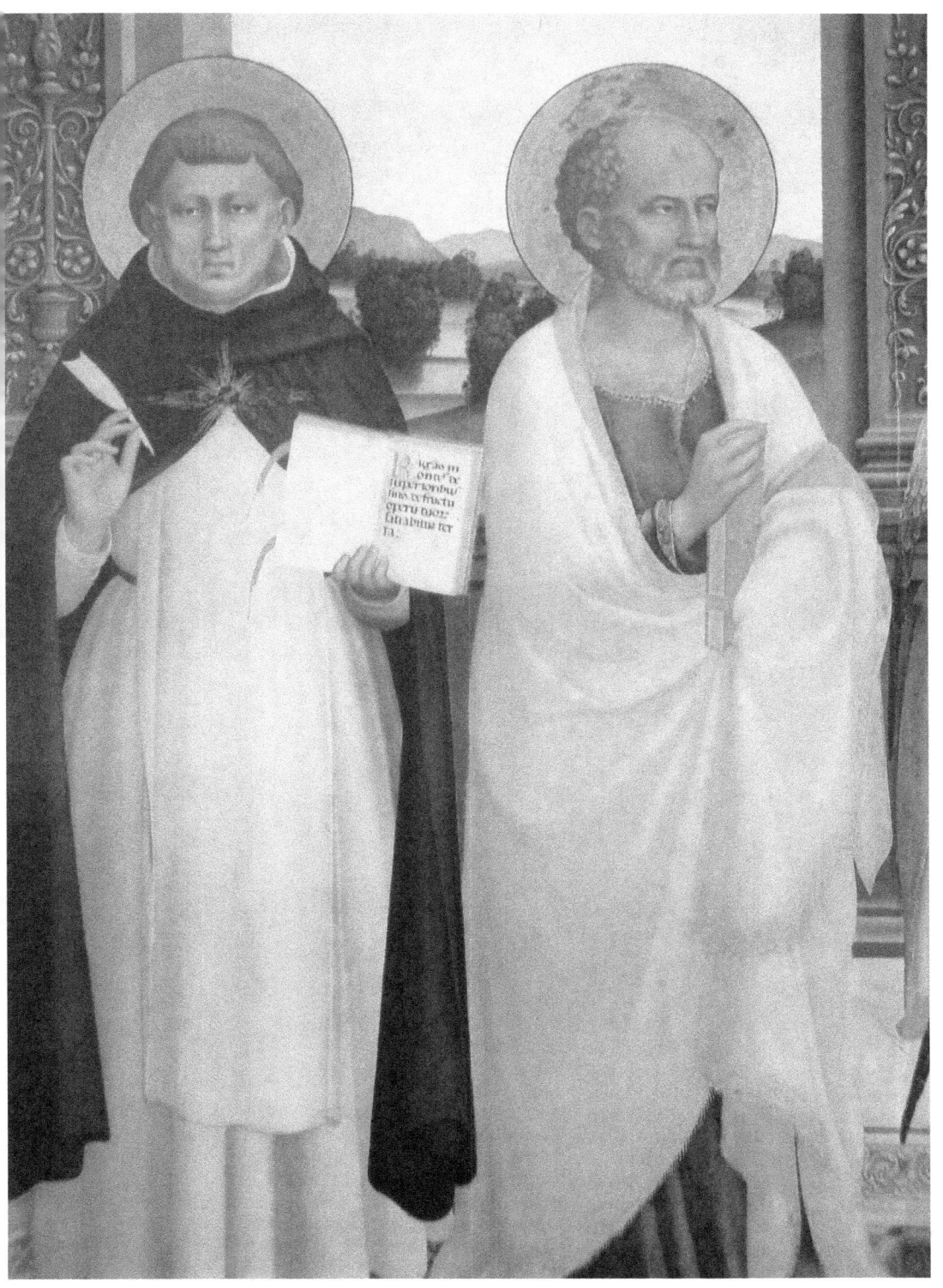

Fra Angelico, Virgin and Child Enthroned, c. 1424-25, detail, Fiesole

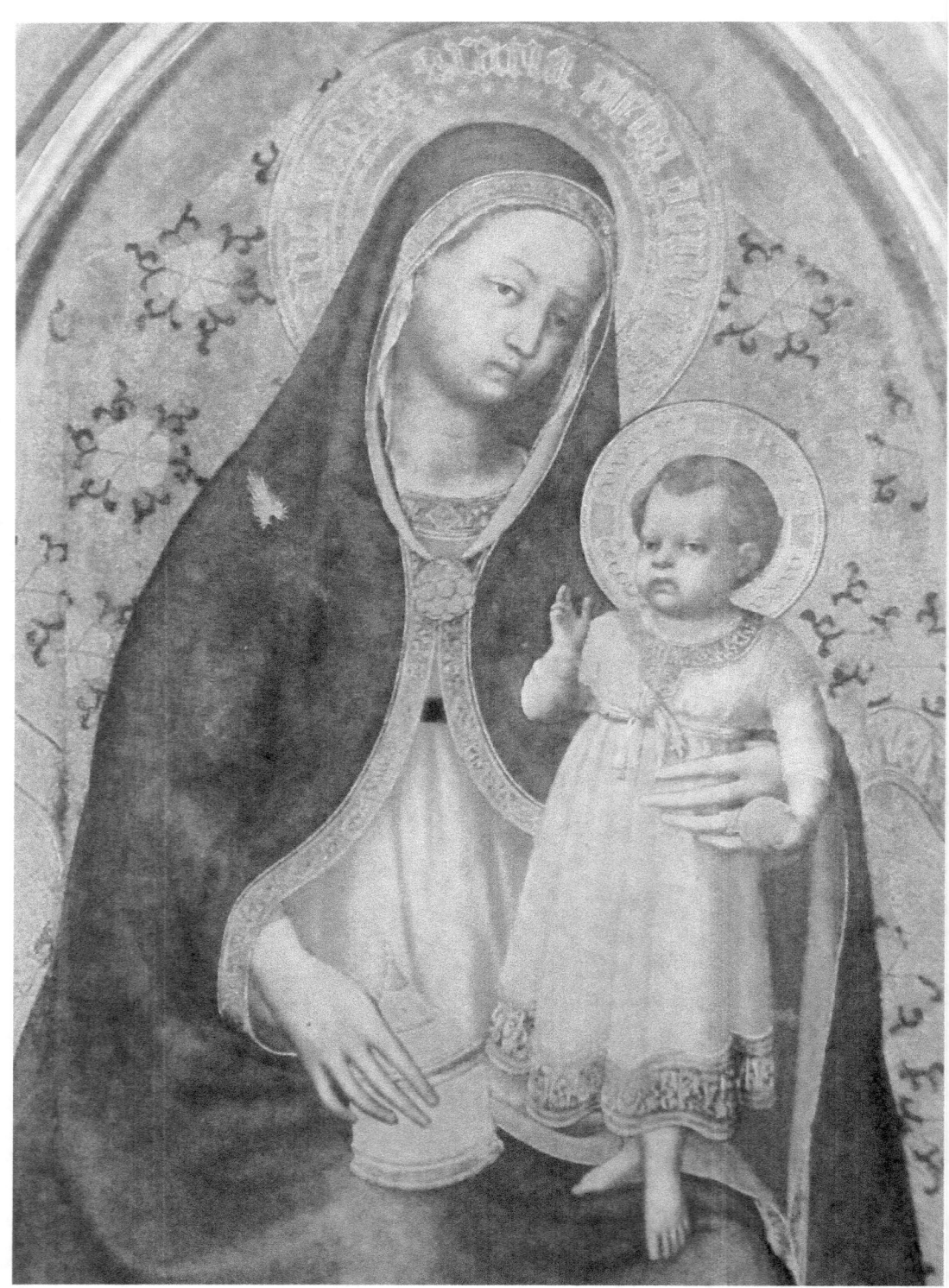

Fra Angelico, San Pier Martire Altarpiece

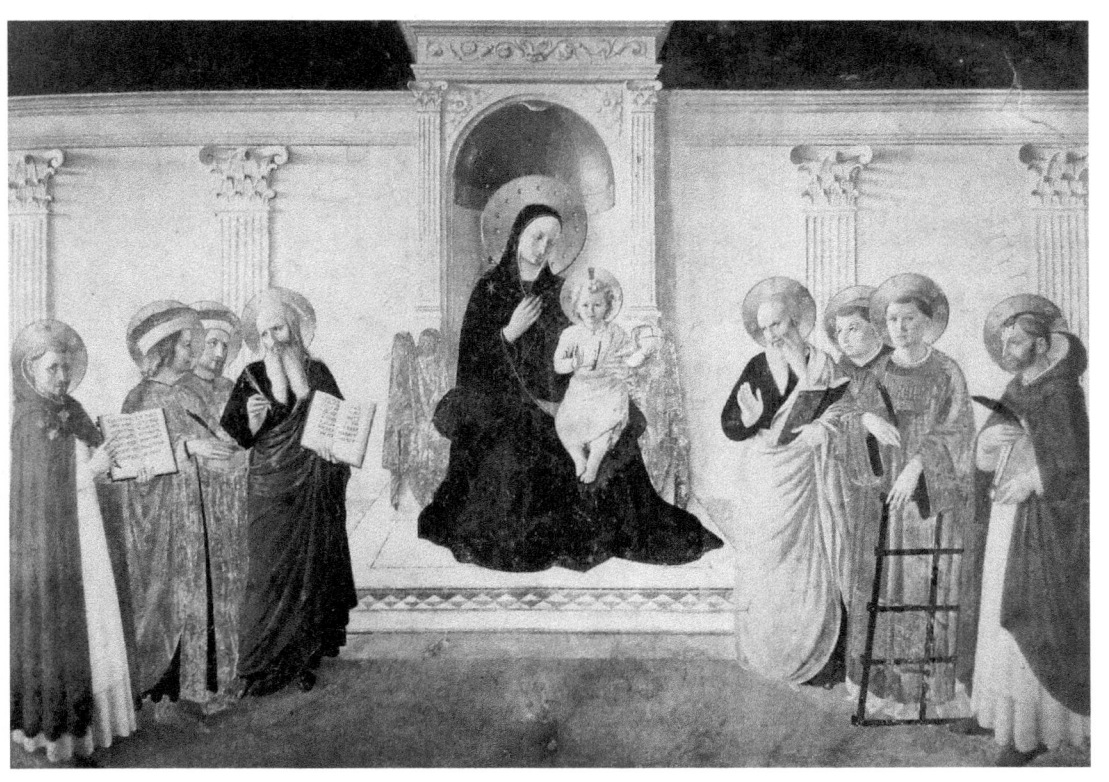

Fra Angelico, Sacra Conversazione, 1440

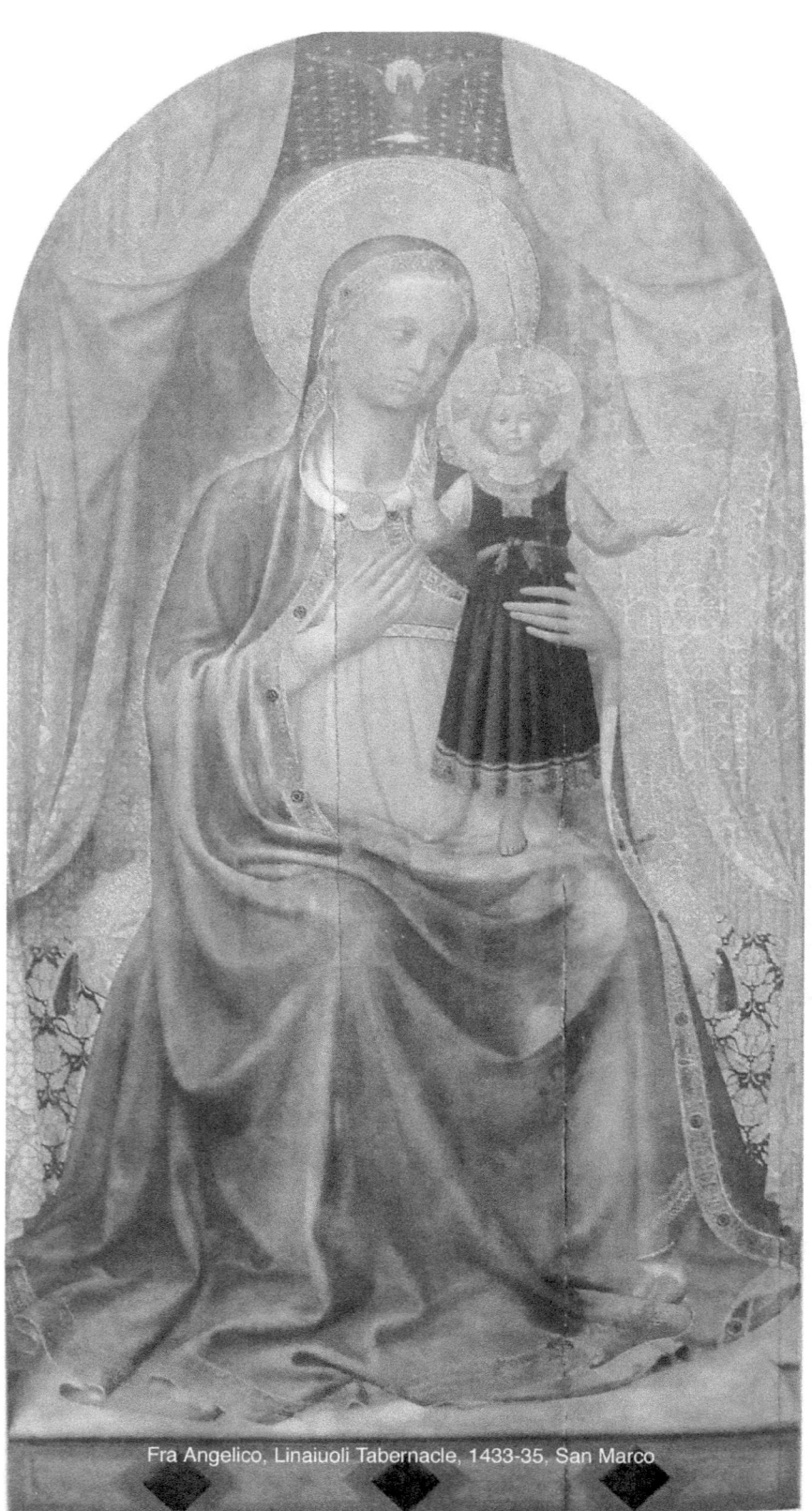

Fra Angelico, Linaiuoli Tabernacle, 1433-35, San Marco

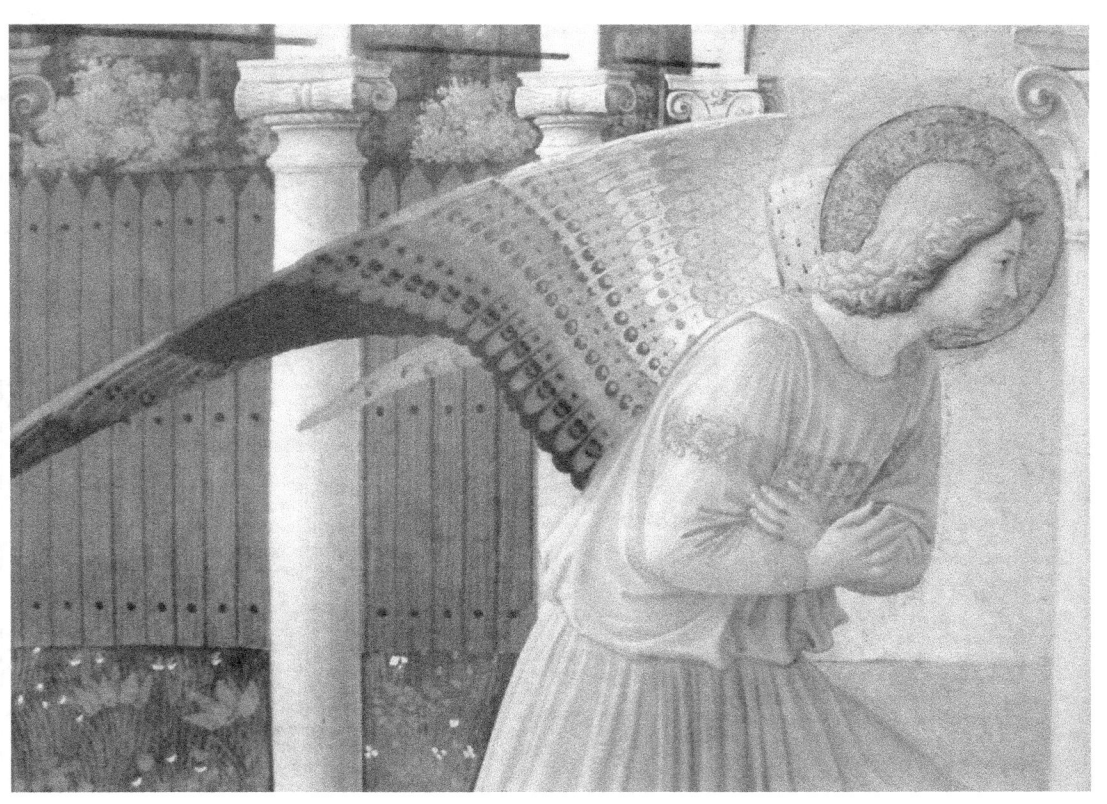

Fra Angelico, Annunciation, c. 1450, detail, upper corridor, San Marco

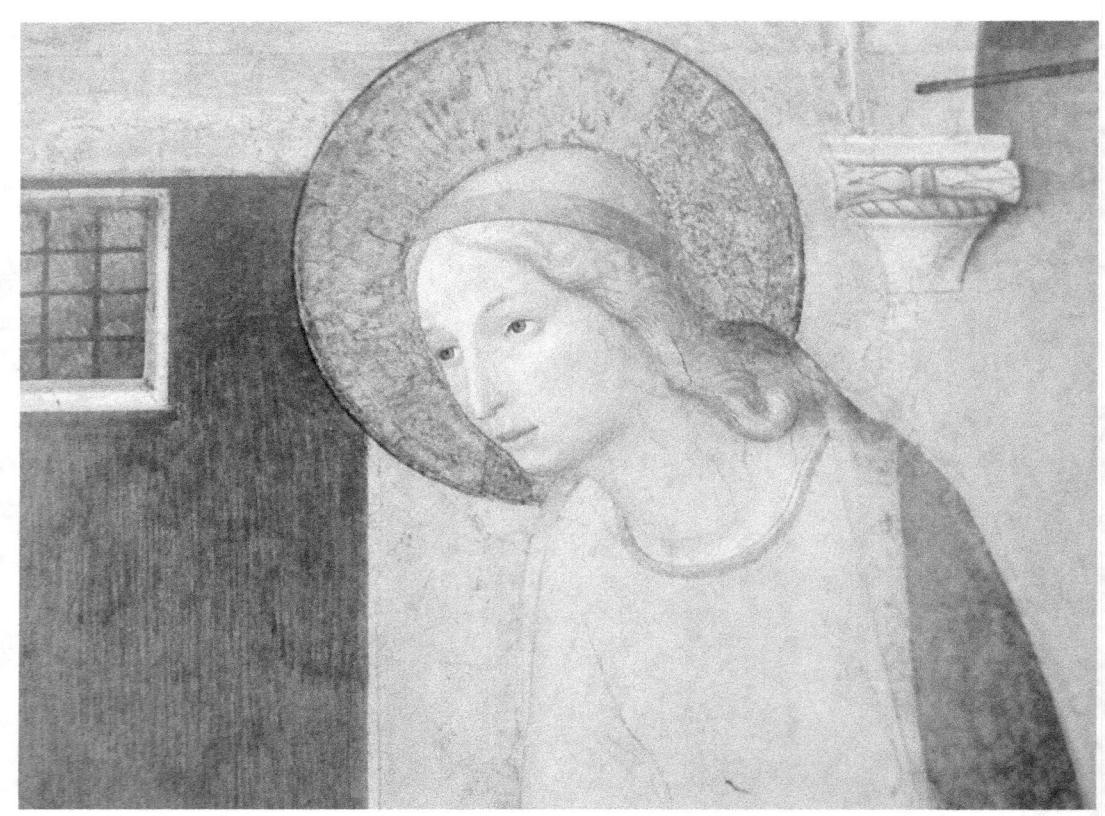

Fra Angelico, Annunciation, detail, San Marco, Florence

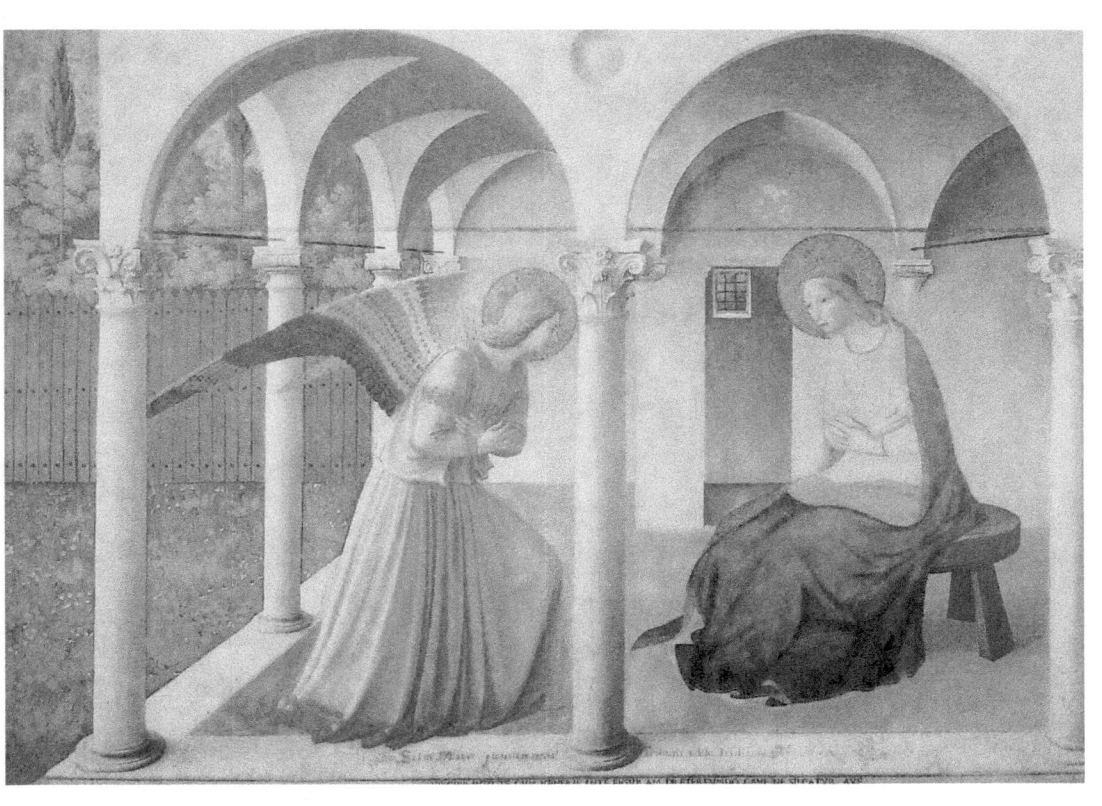

Fra Angelico, The Annunciation, San Marco, Florence

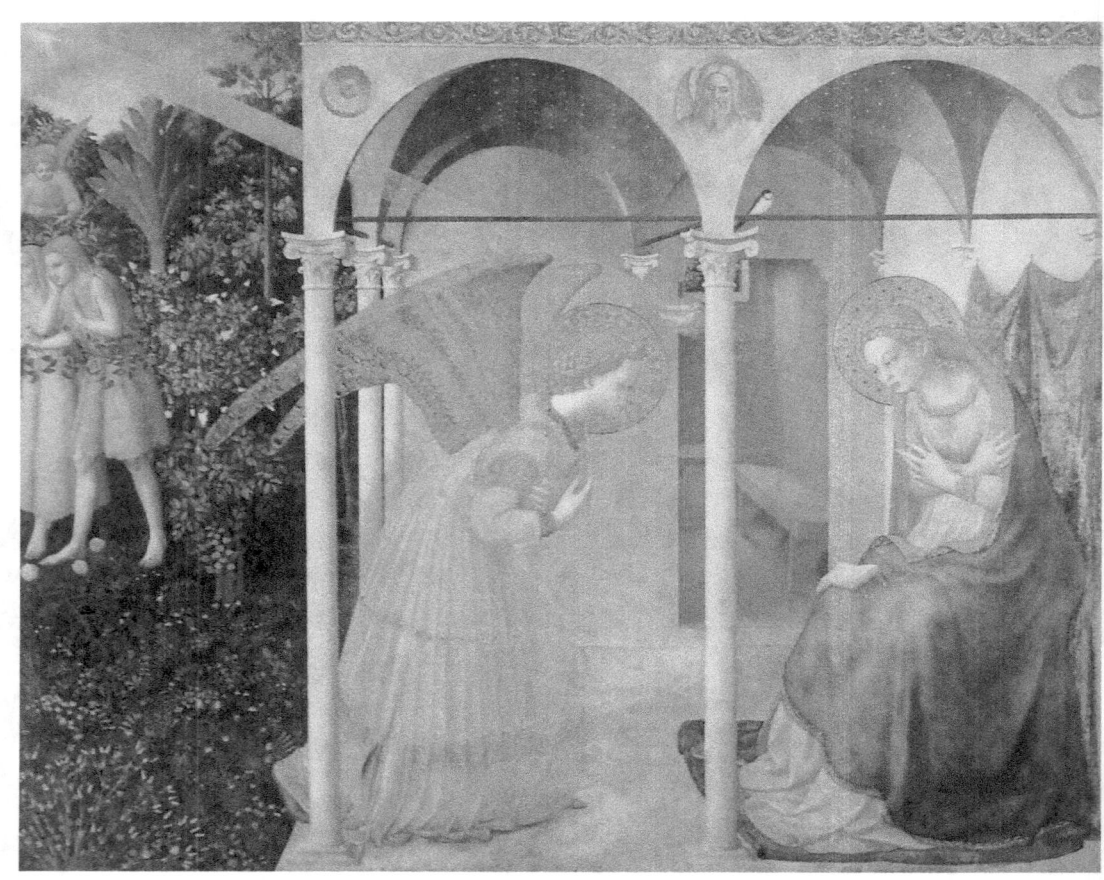

Fra Angelico, Annunciation, Prado, Madrid

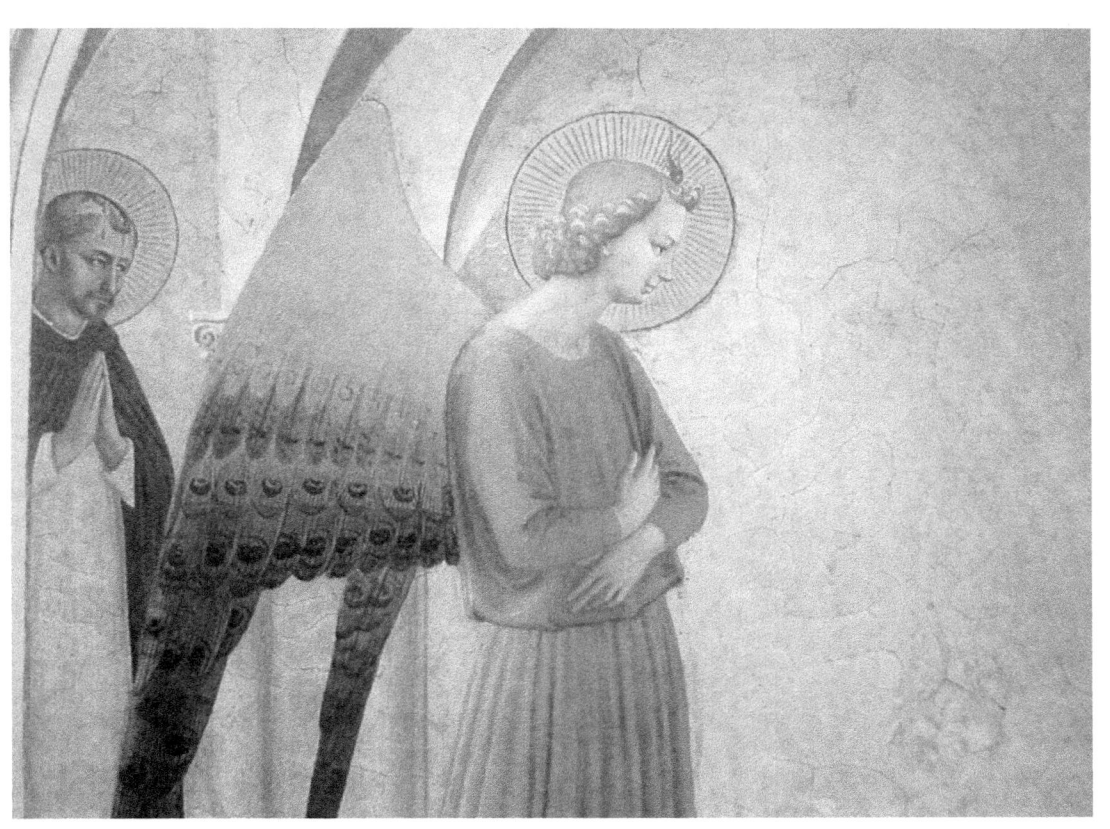

Fra Angelico, Annunciation, cell 3, San Marco

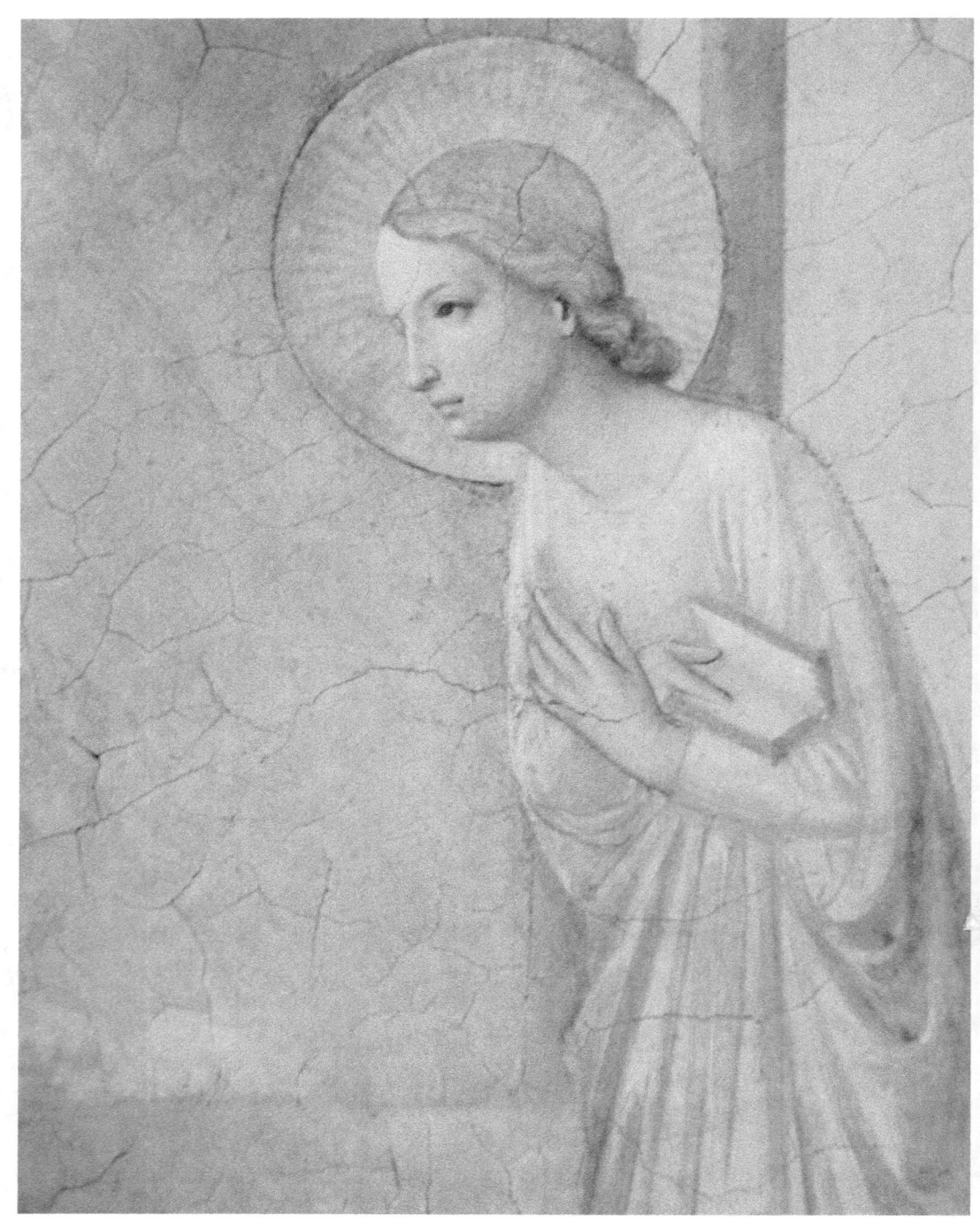

Fra Angelico, Annunciation, cell 3 at San Marco

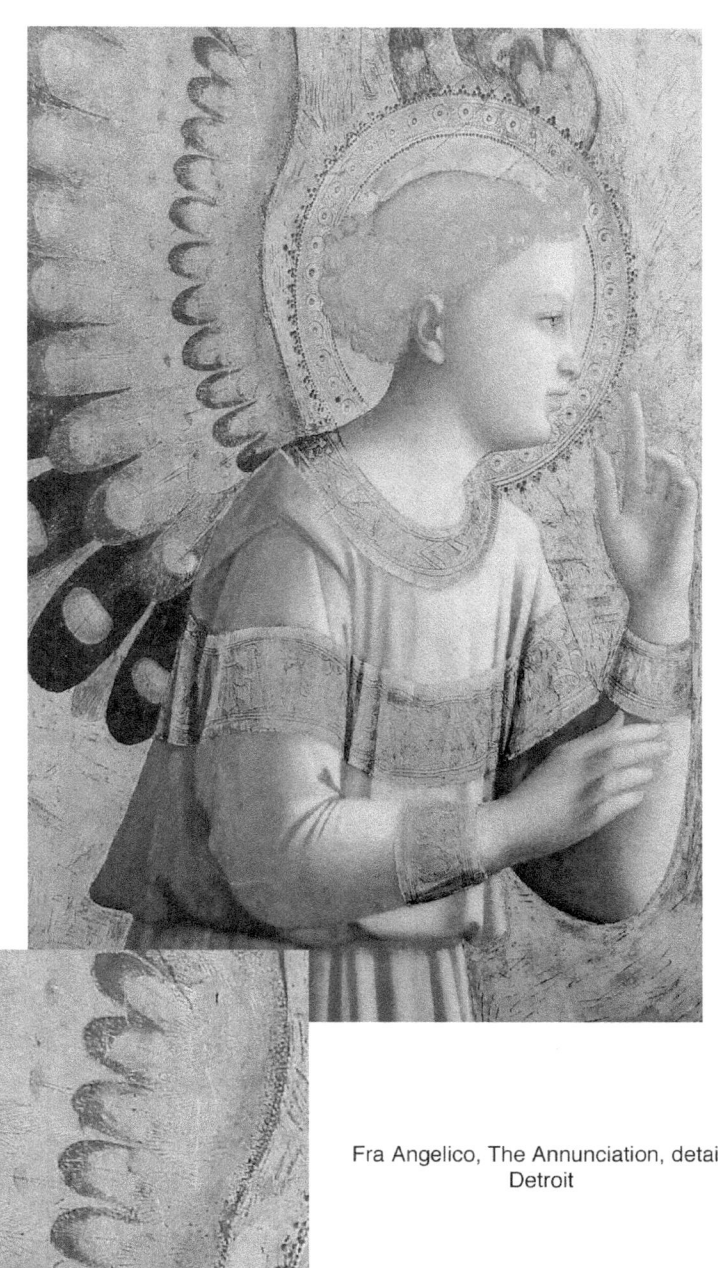

Fra Angelico, The Annunciation, detail,
Detroit

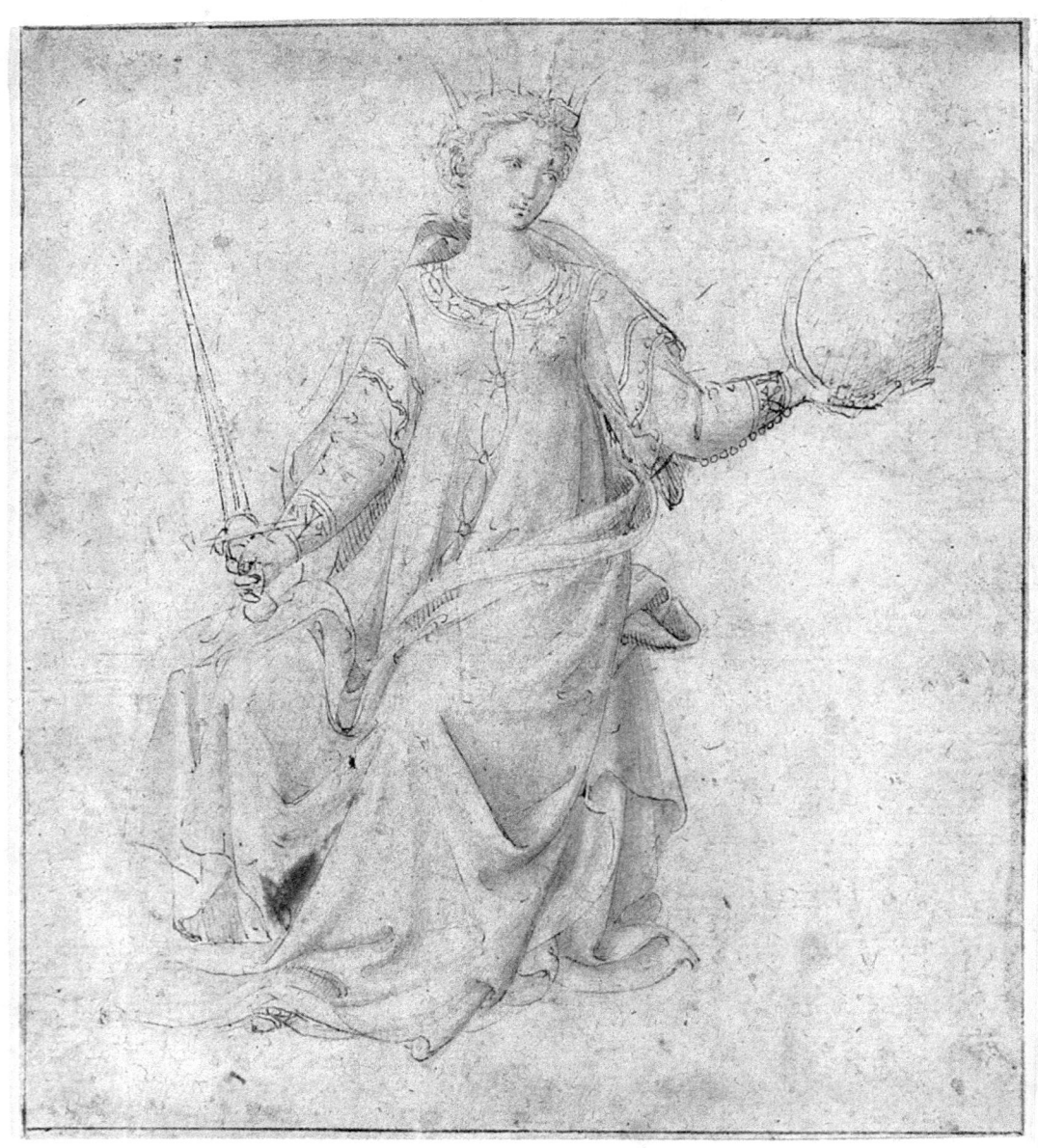

Fra Angelico, Justice, Metropolitan Museum of Art, NYC

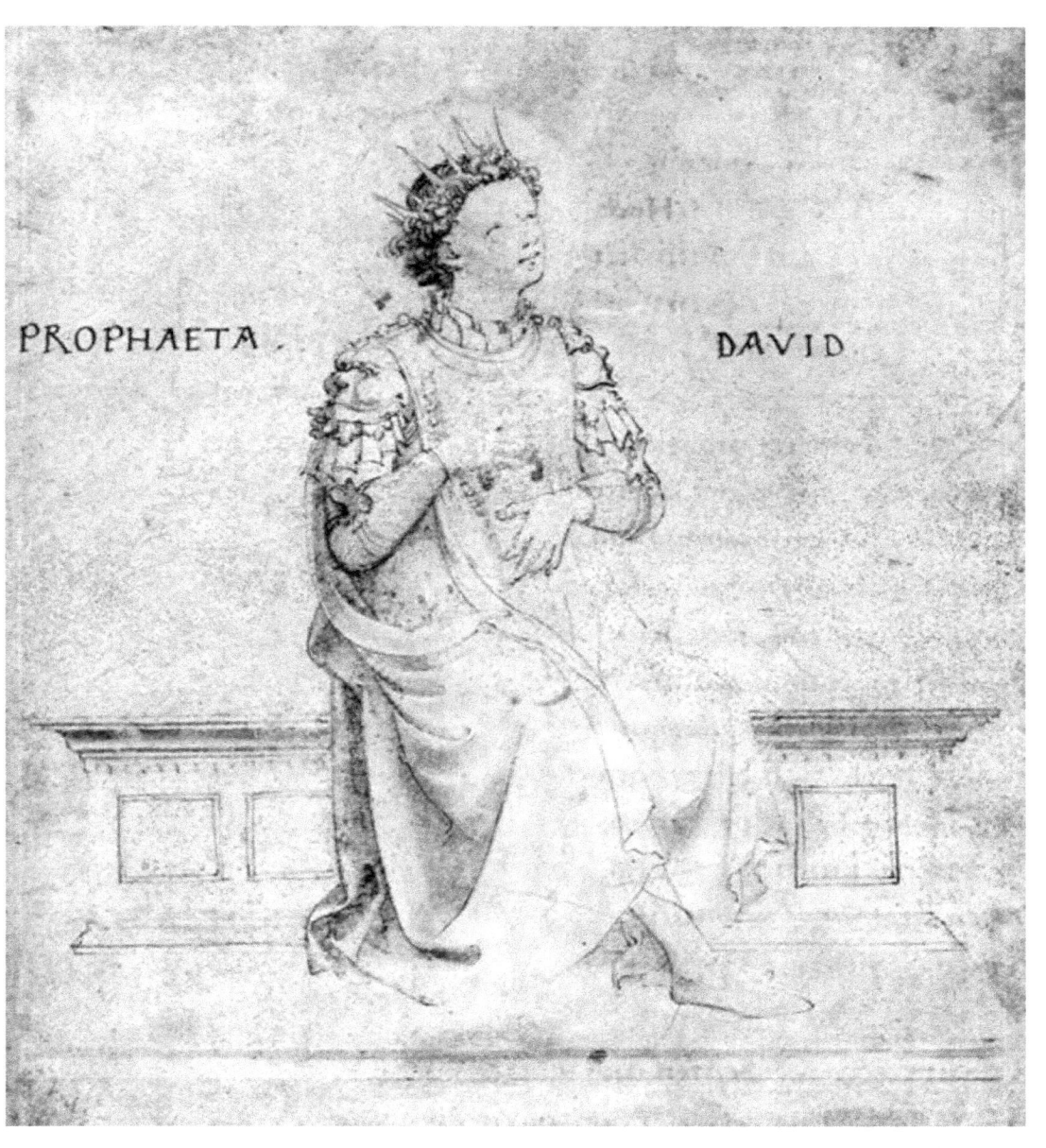

PROPHAETA . DAVID

Fra Angelico, King David, 1430, San Marco

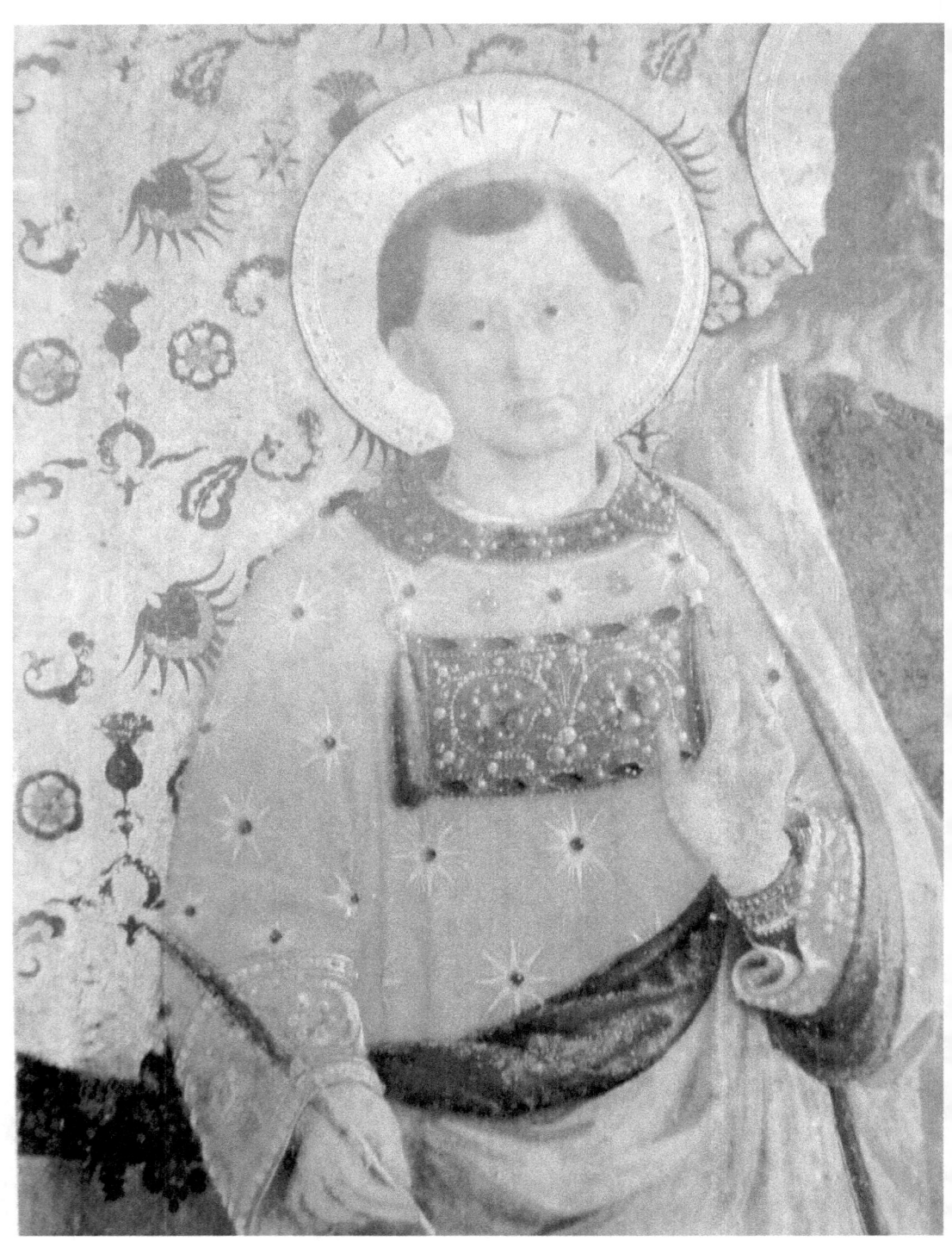

Fra Angelico, San Marco Altarpiece, 1438-40, detail

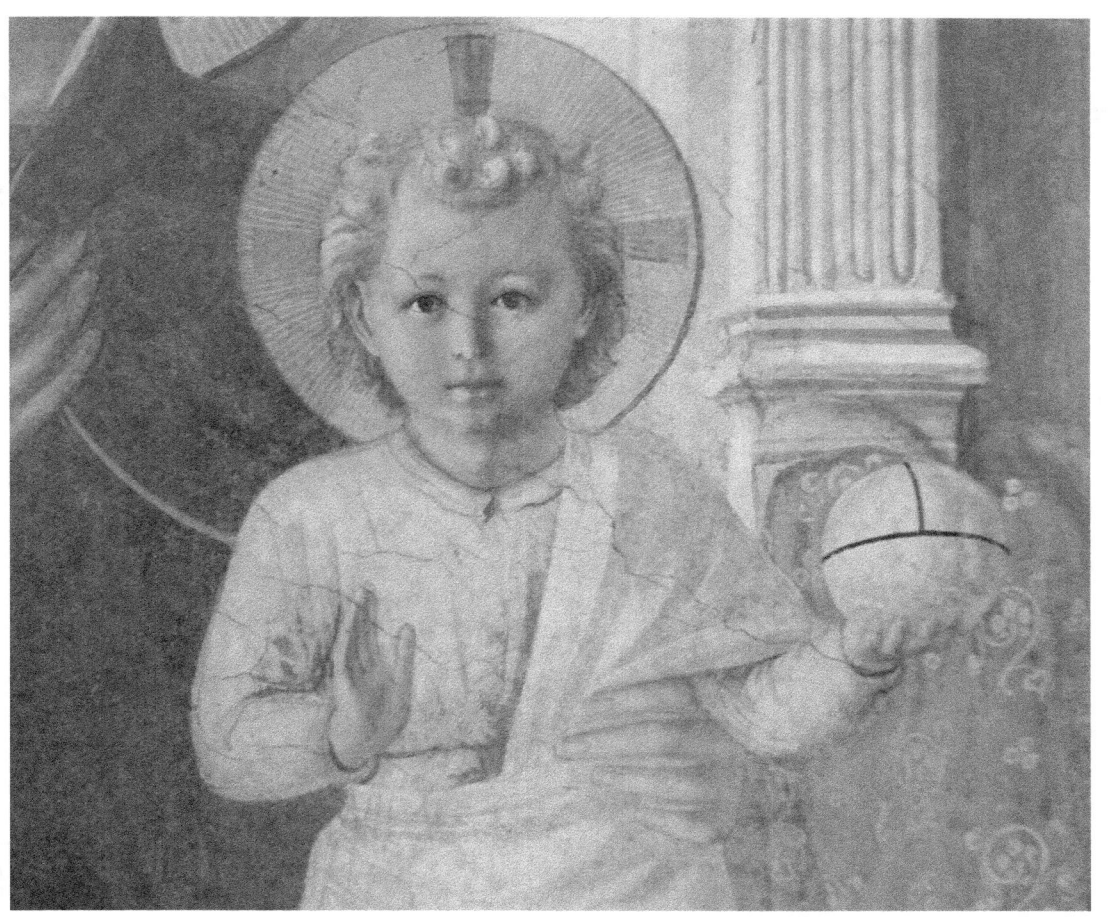

Fra Angelico, Virgin and Child Enthroned, c. 1450, detail, San Marco

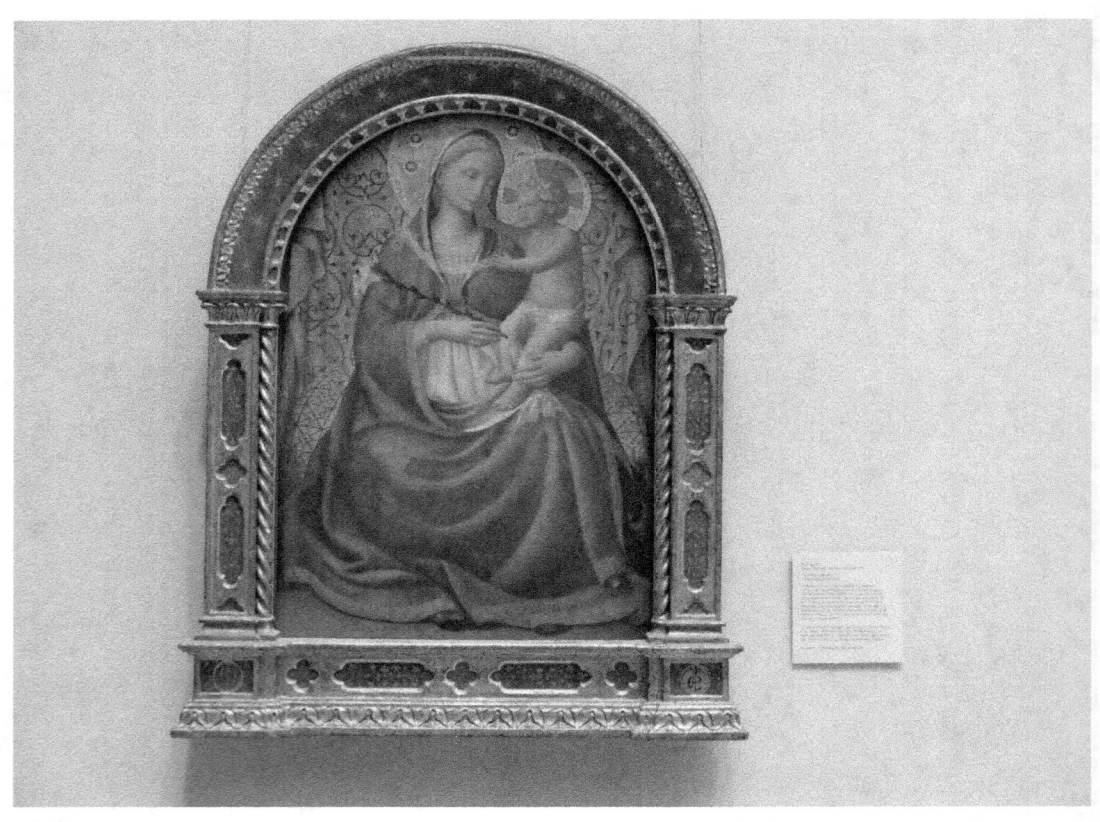

Fra Angelico, Madonna and Child, Metropolitan Museum of Art, New York

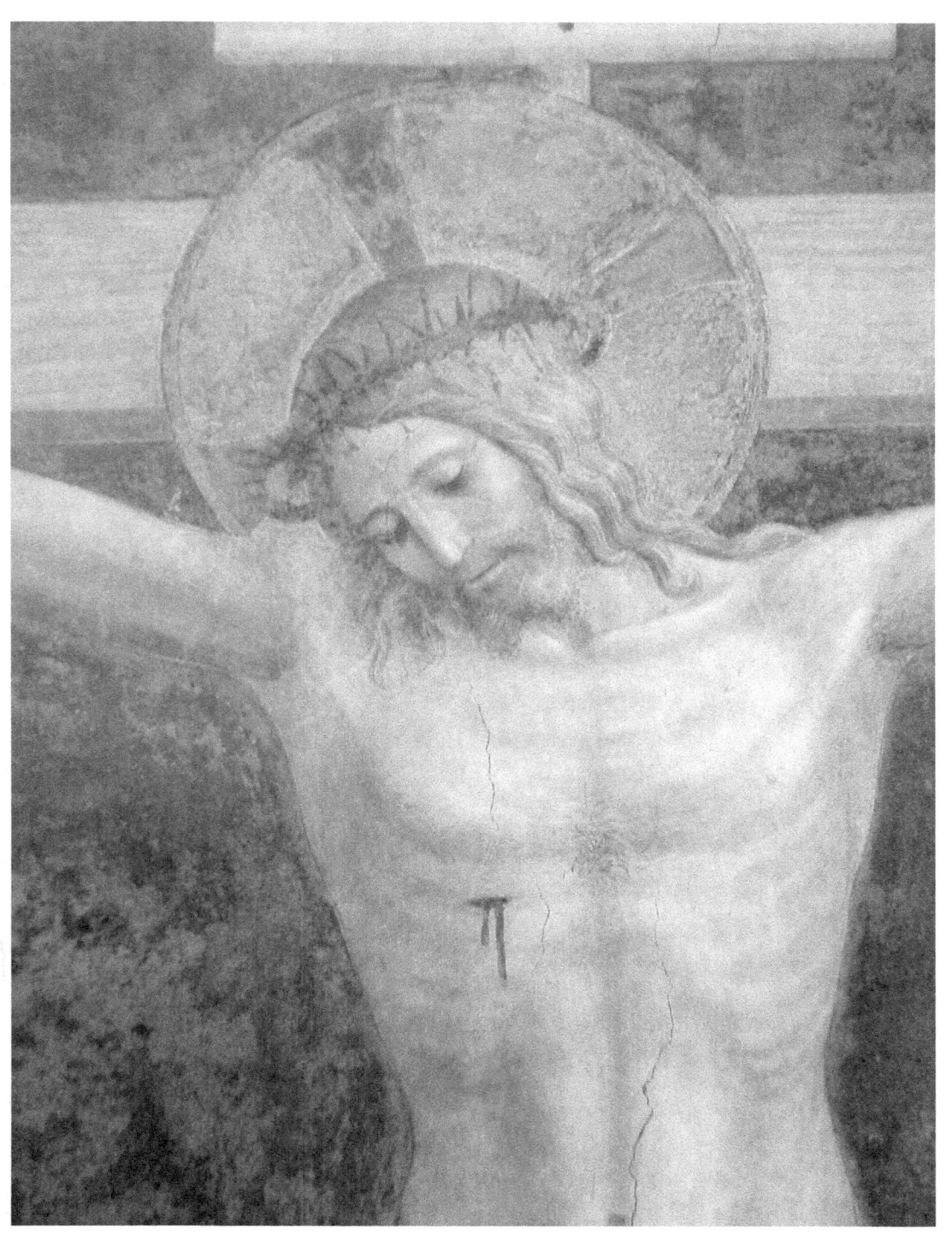

Fra Angelico, Christ On the Cross, c. 1442, detail, San Marco

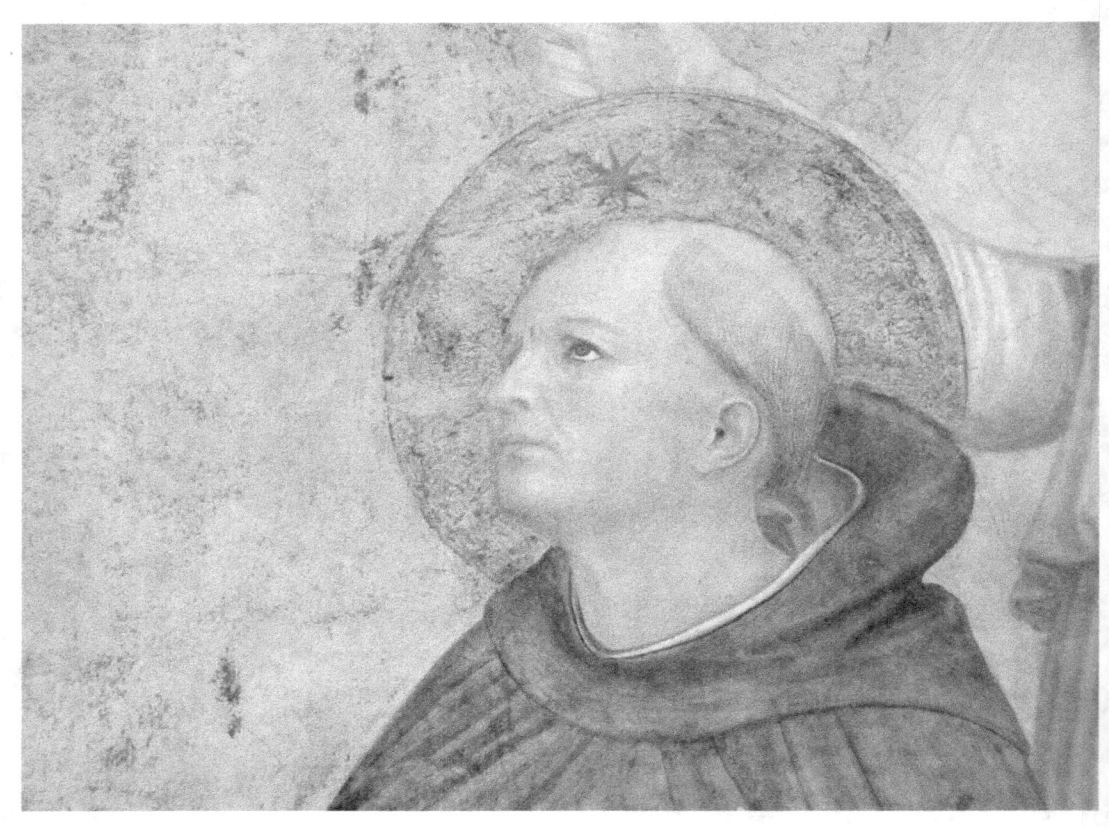

Fra Angelico, Crucifixion, detail, 1441-42, San Marco

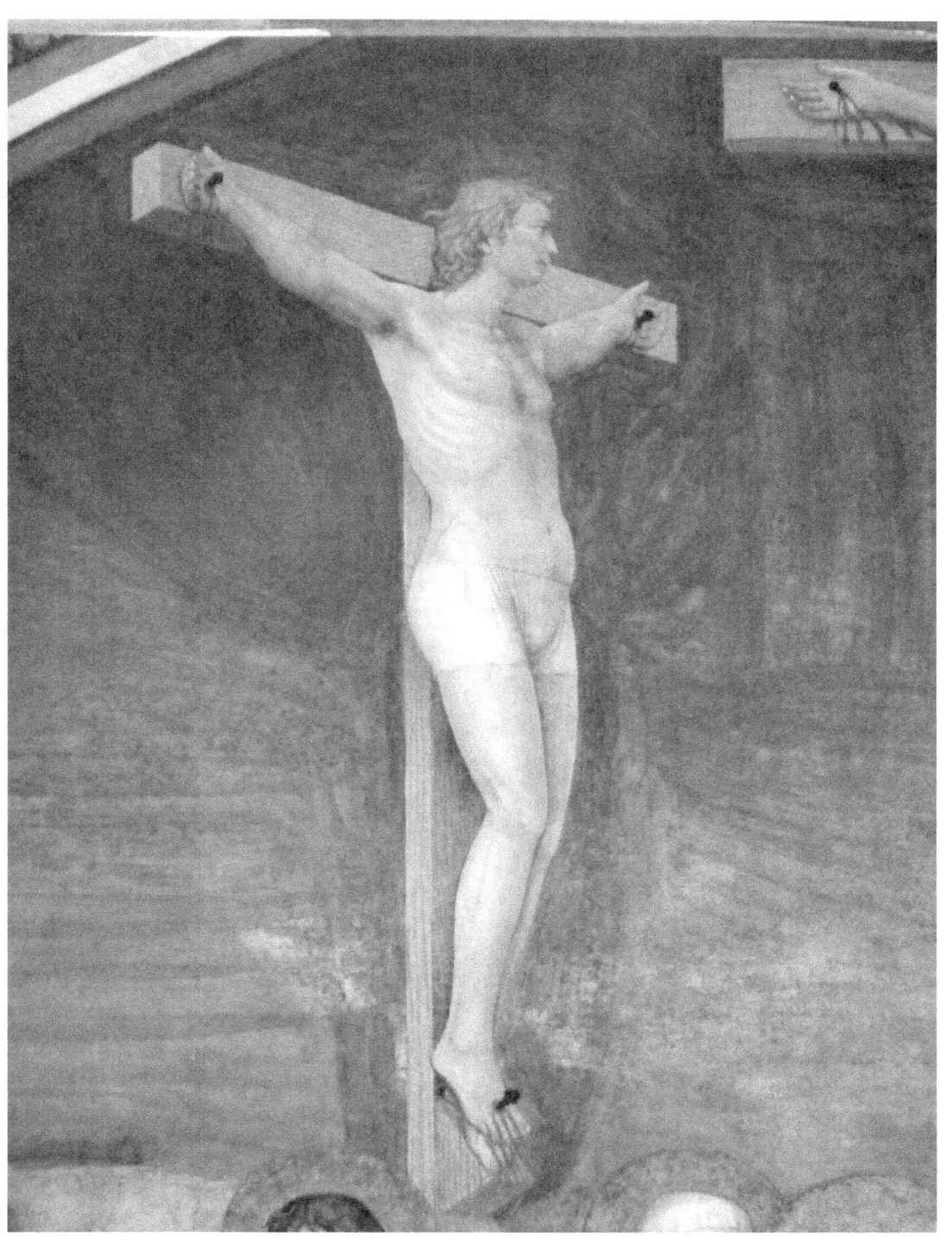

Fra Angelico, Crucifixion, 1441-42, San Marco, detail

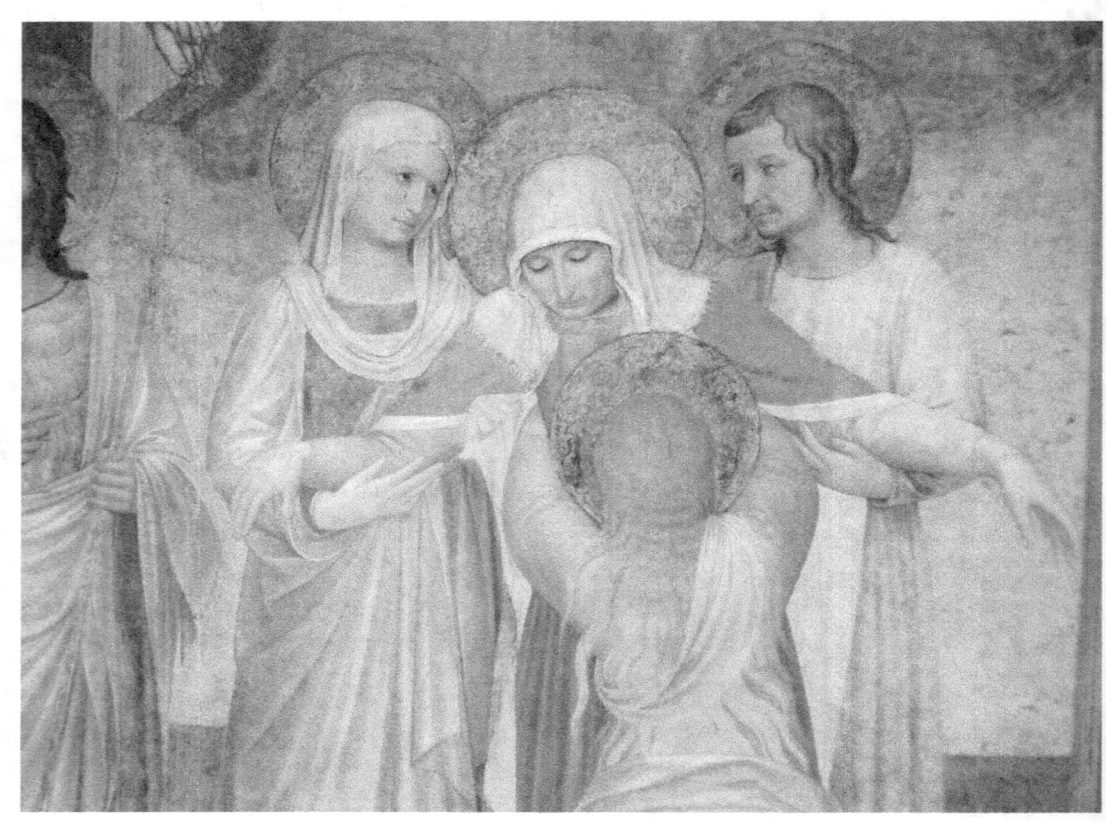

Fra Angelico, Crucifixion, detail

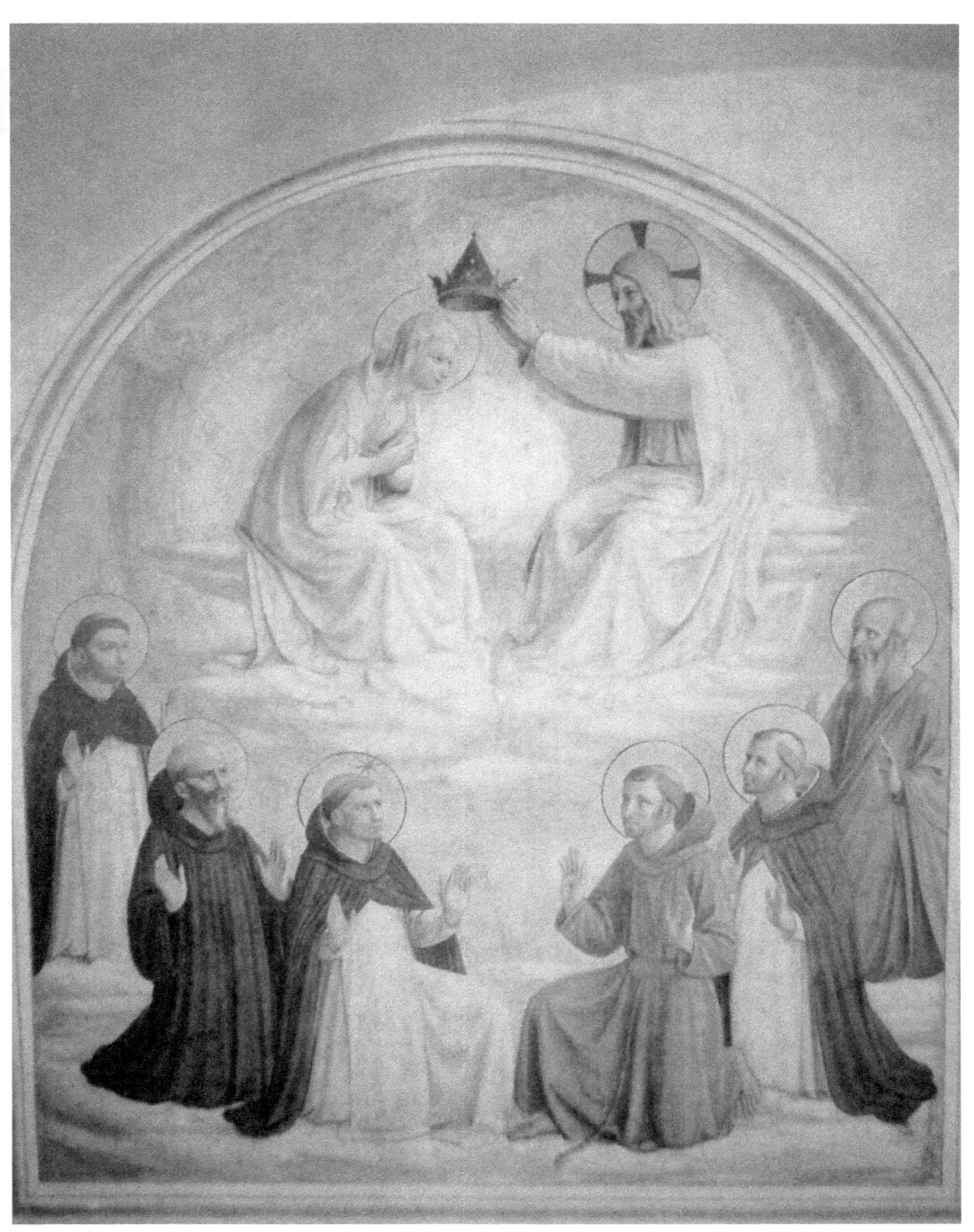

Fra Angelico, The Coronation of the Virgin, San Marco

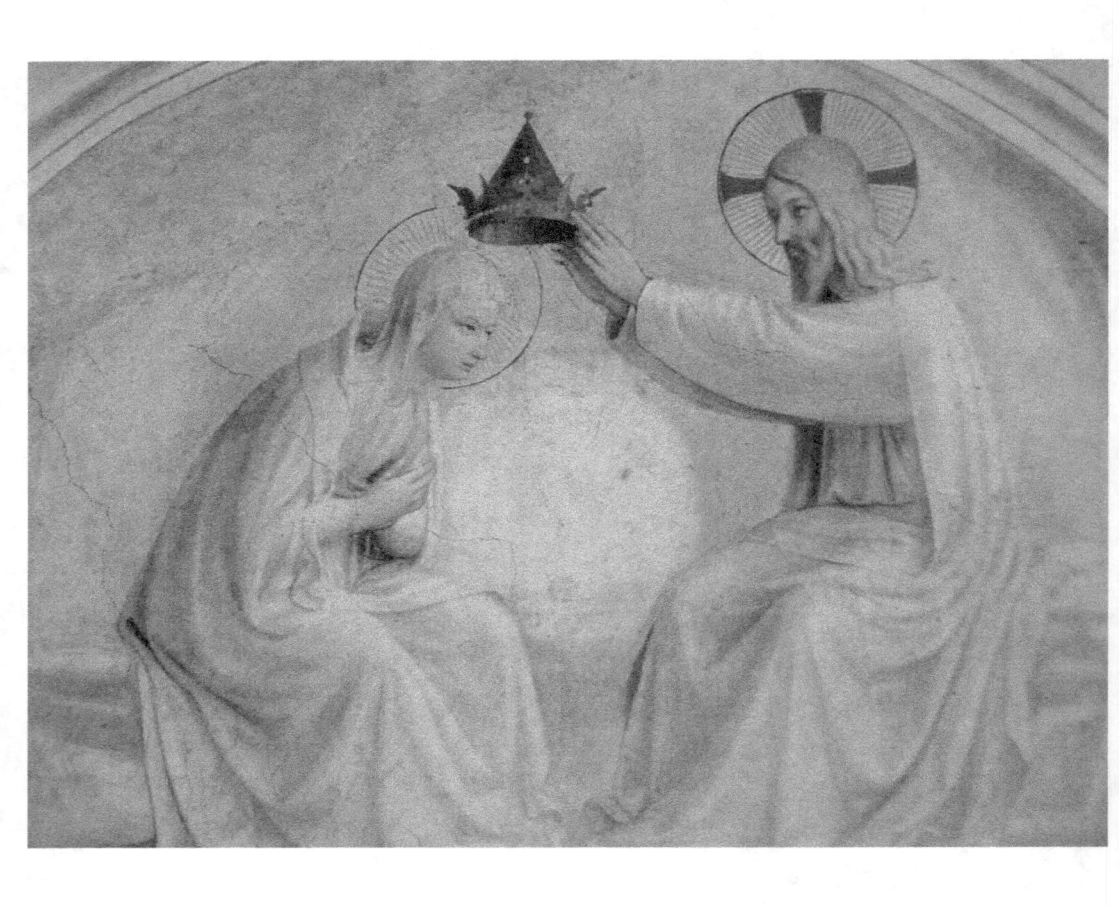

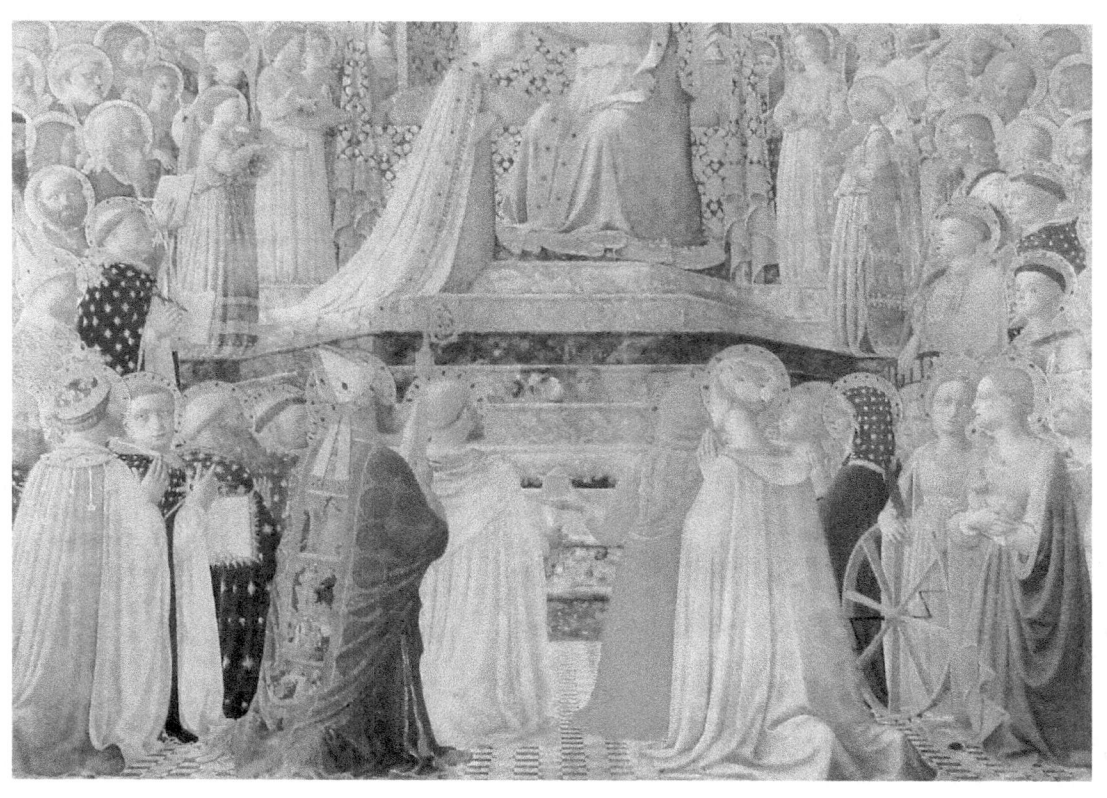

Fra Angelico, The Coronation of the Virgin, Louve, Paris, detail

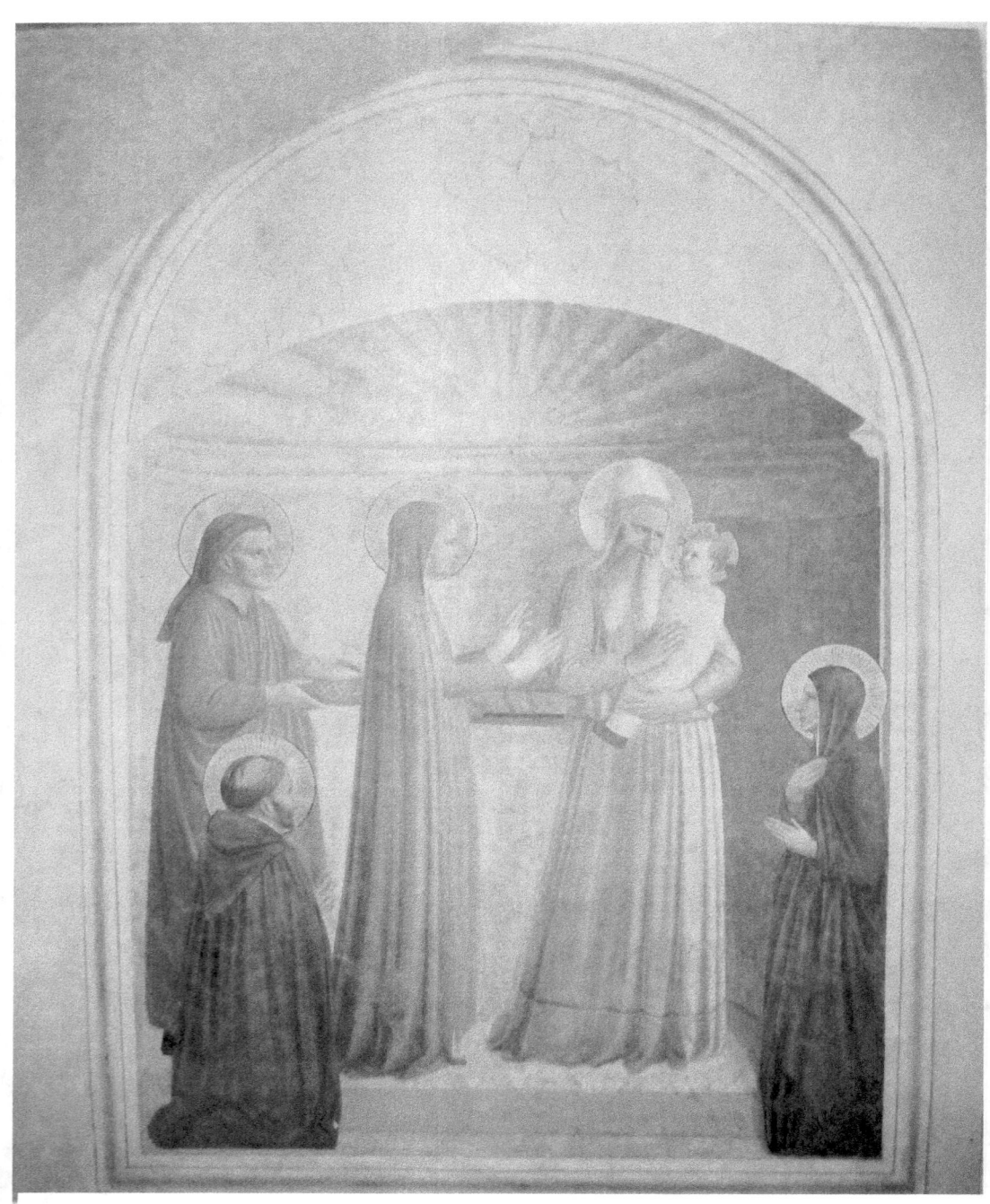

Fra Angelico, Presentation In the Temple, San Marco

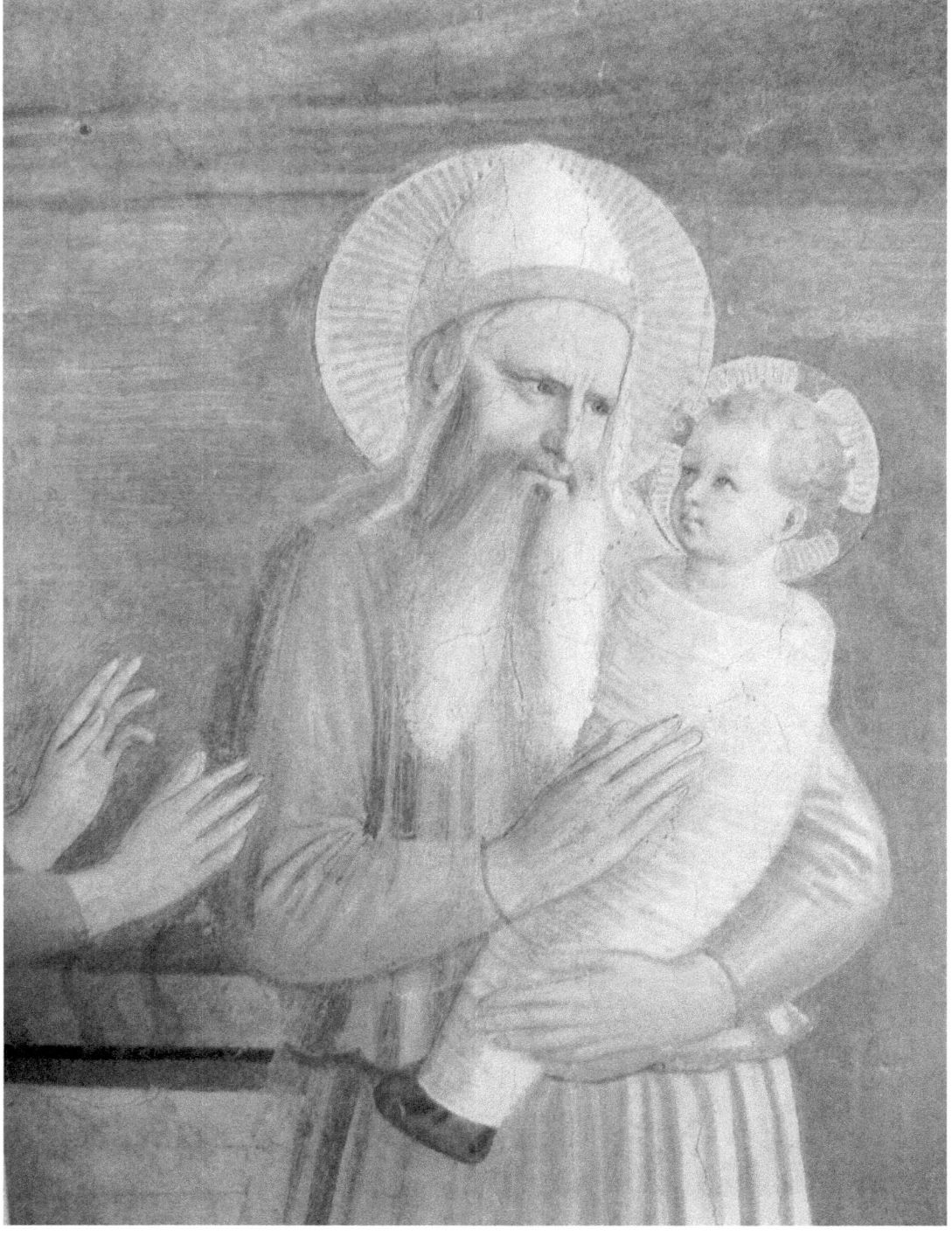

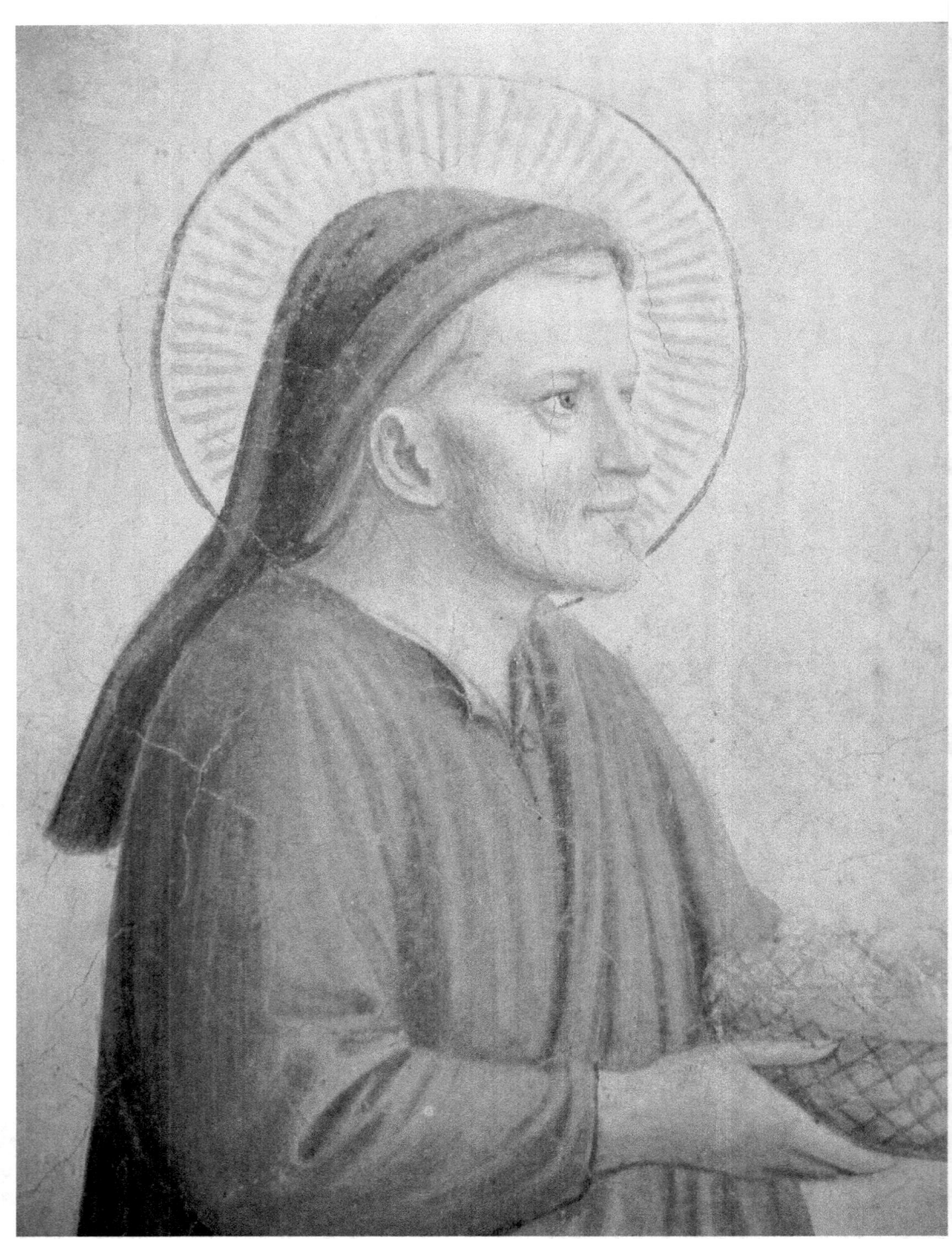

Fra Angelico, Presentation In the Temple, 1440-41, San Marco

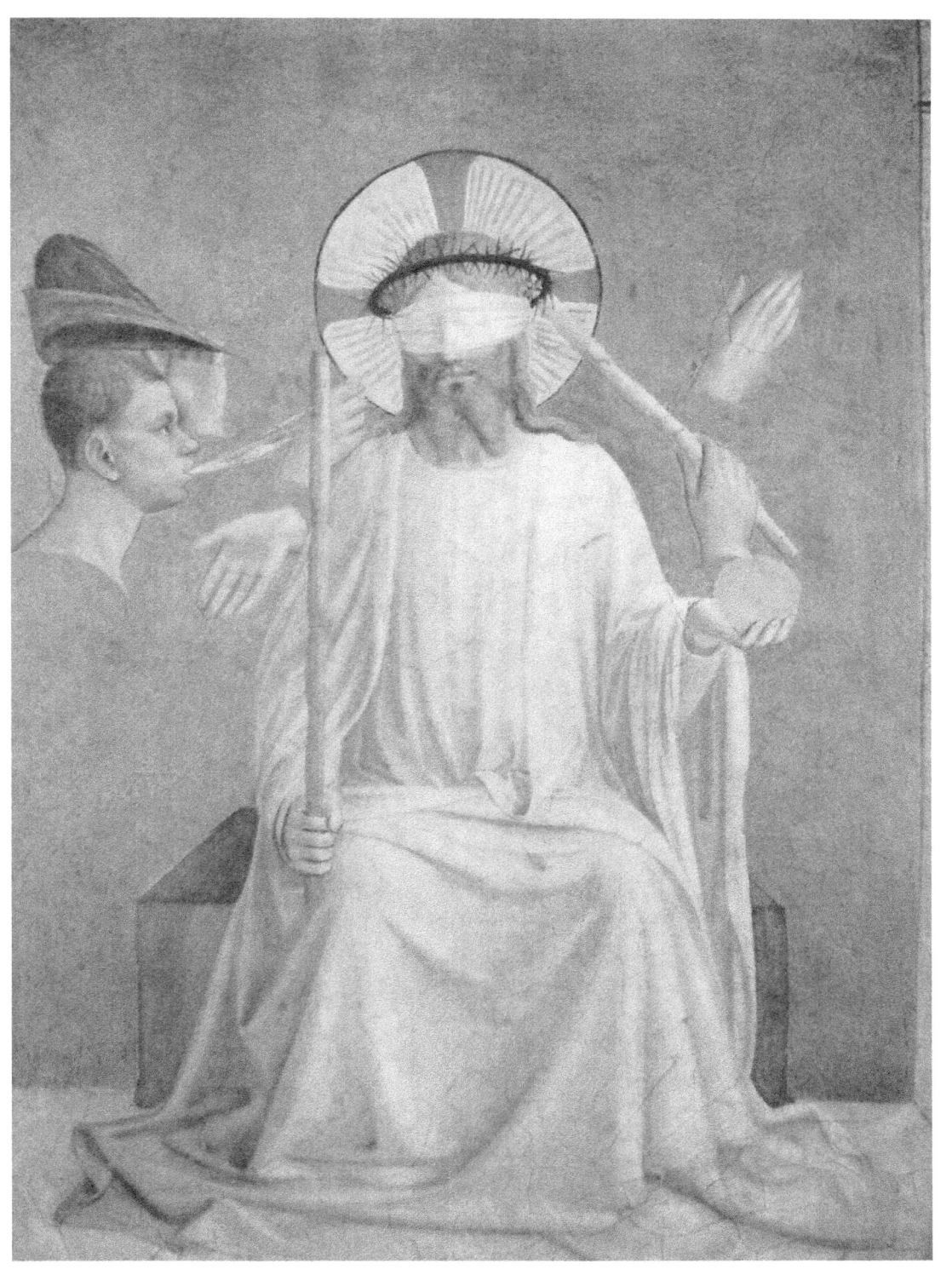

Fra Angelico, The Mocking of Christ, San Marco

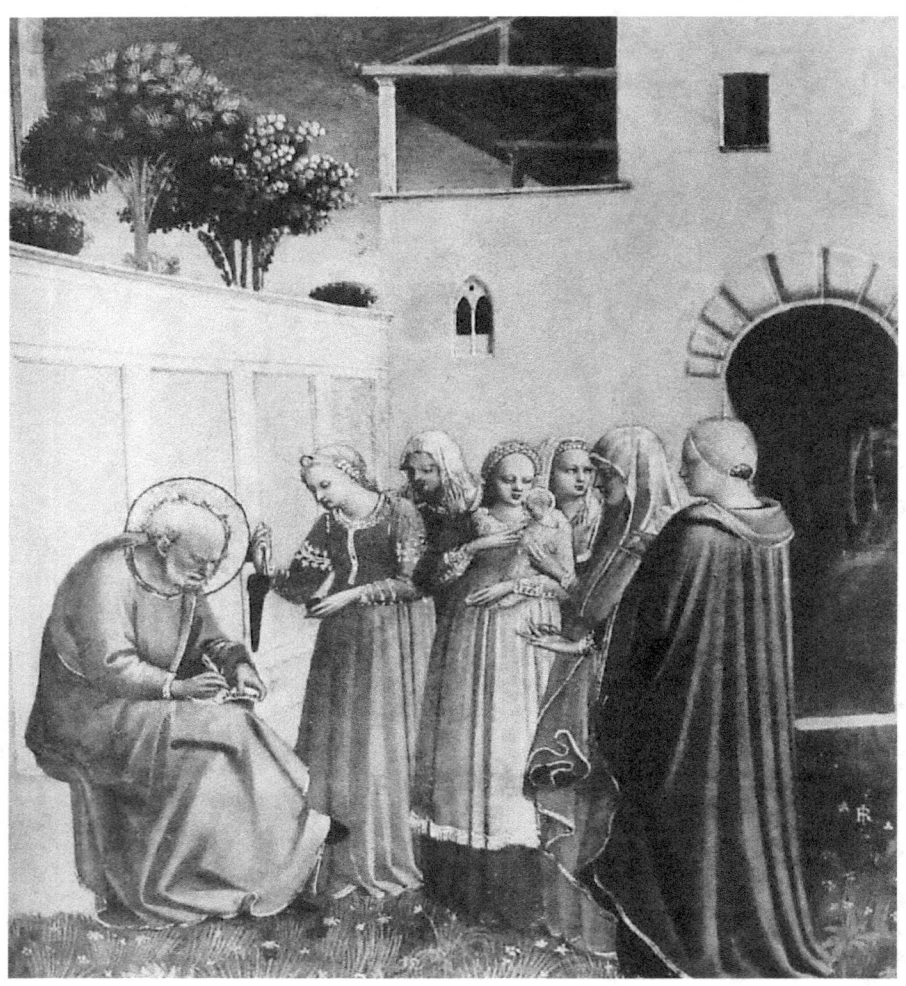

Fra Angelico, The Naming of John the Baptist, 1435

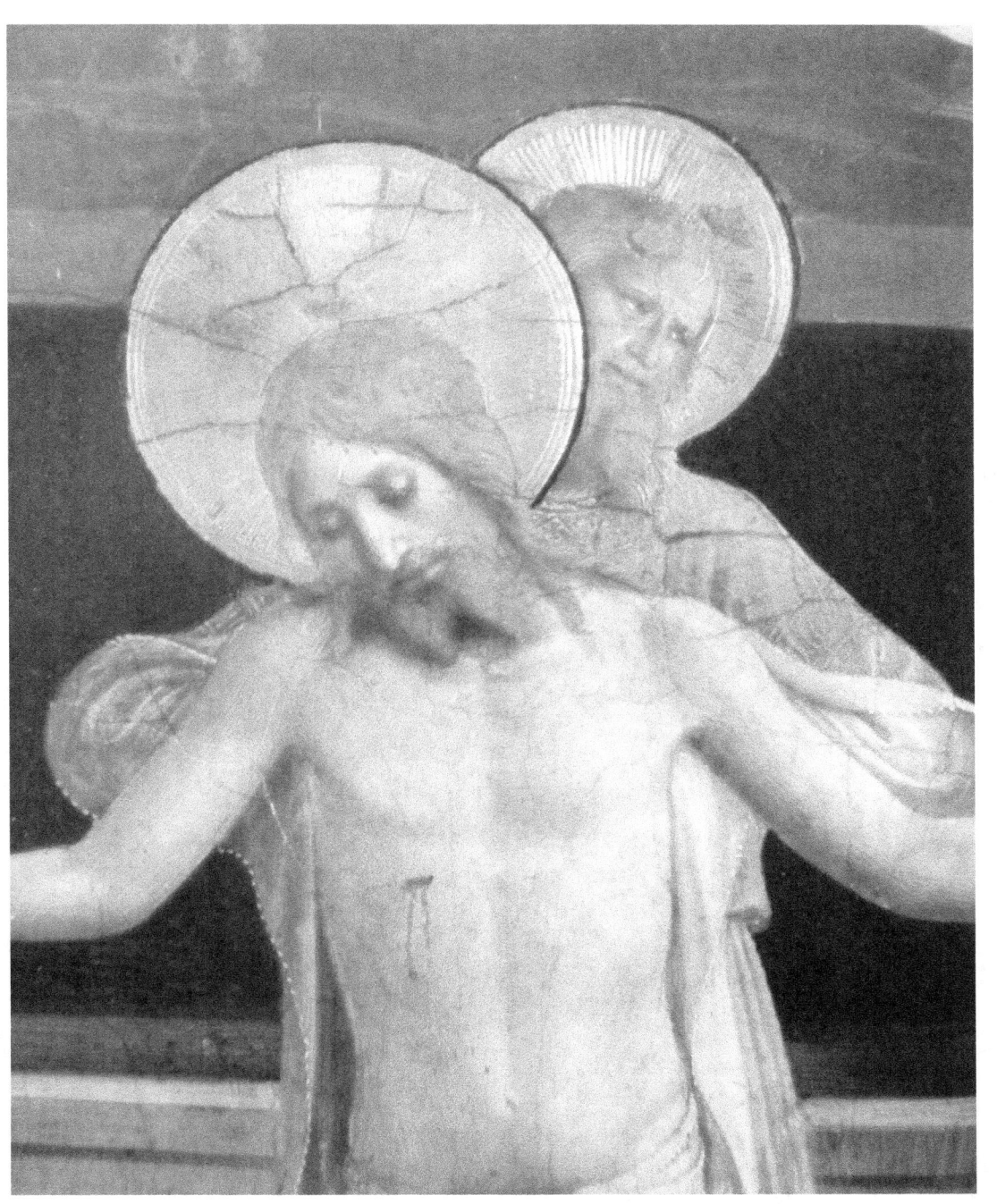

Fra Angelico, Lamentation Over the Dead Christ,
Alte Pinakothek, Munich, detail

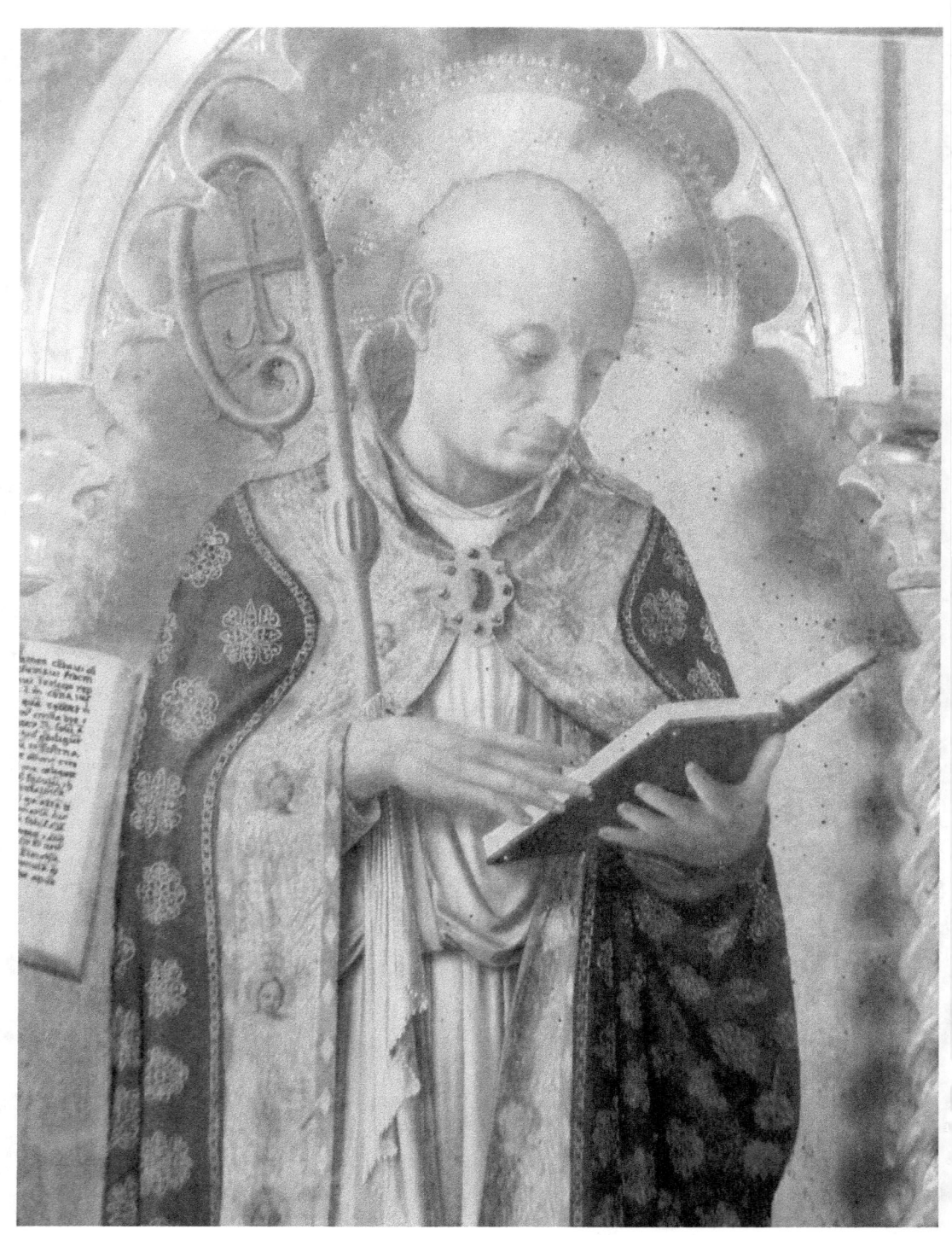

Fra Angelico, Perugia Altarpiece, 1448, detail

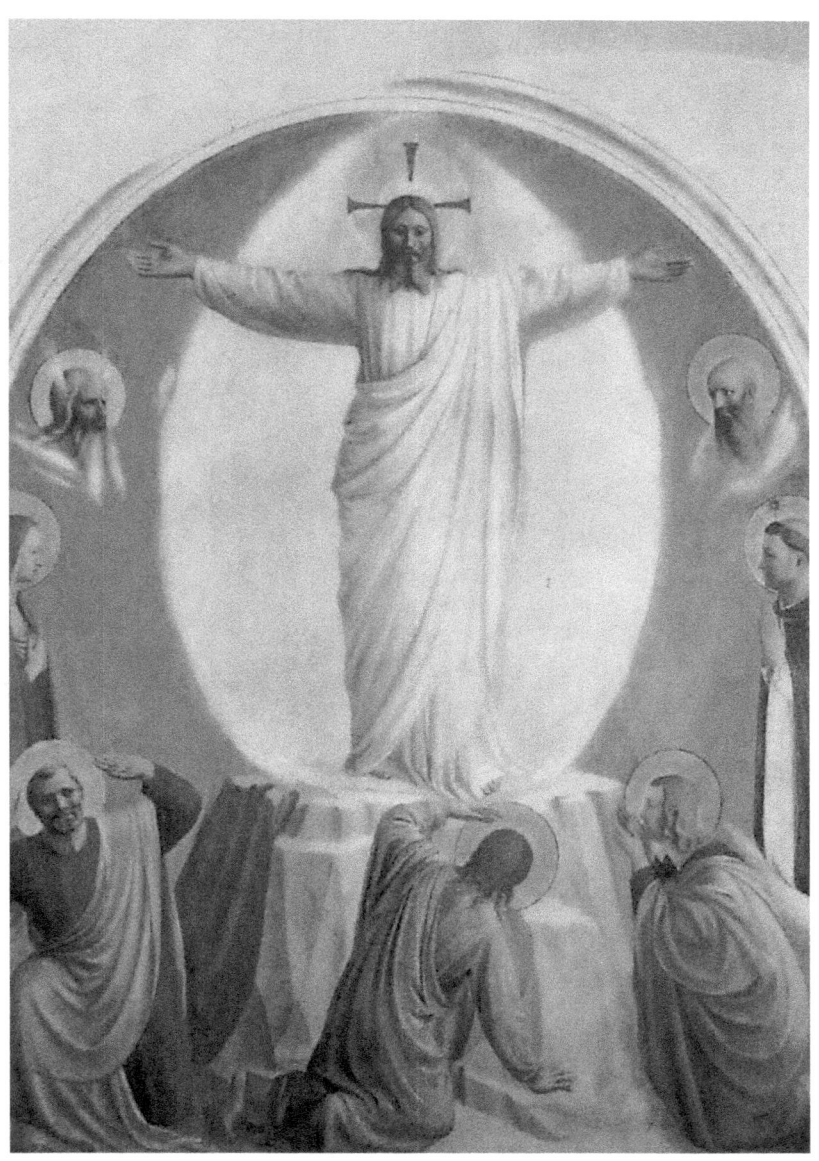

Fra Angelico, The Resurrection, San Marco, Florence

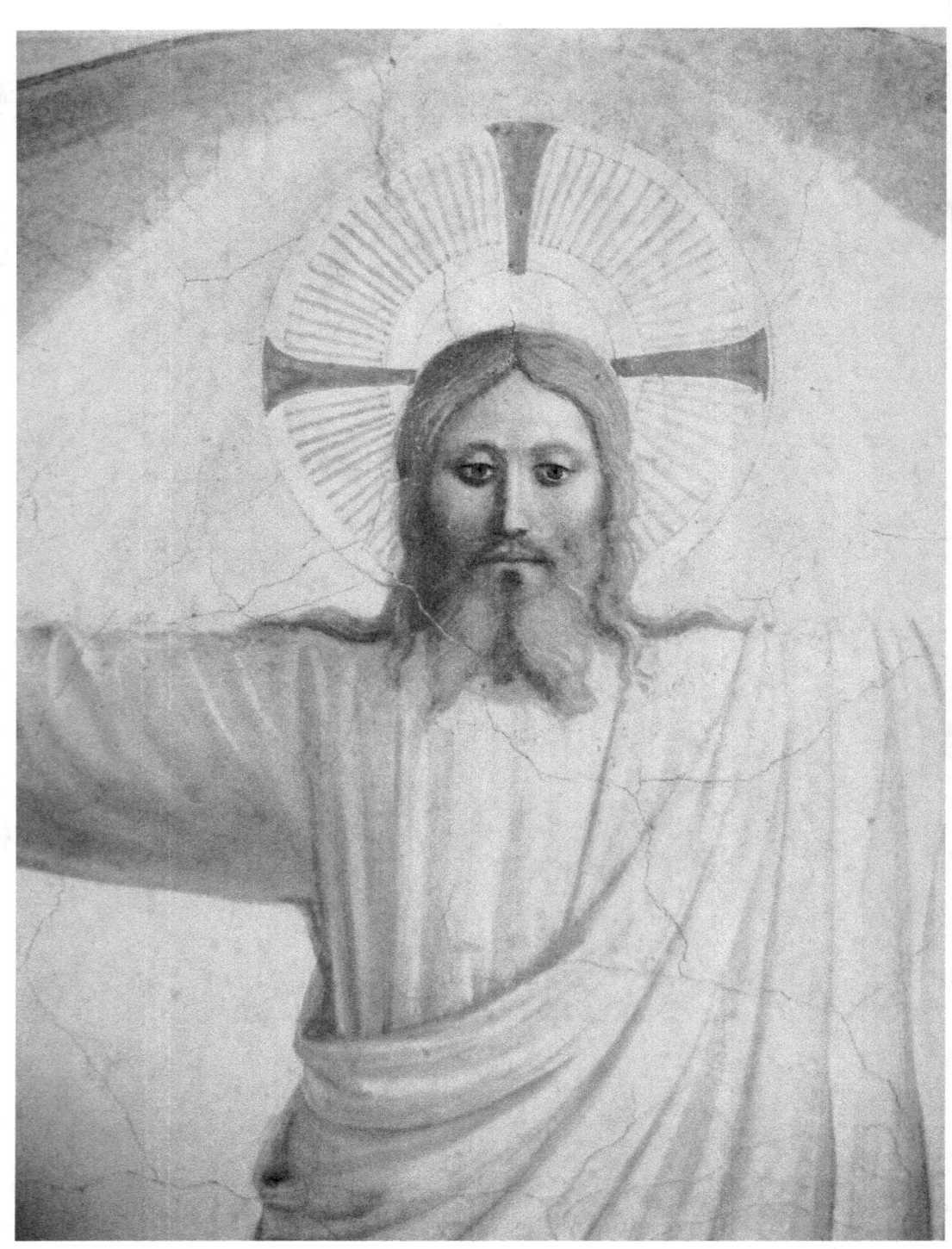

Fra Angelico, The Transfiguration, 1440-41, San Marco, detail

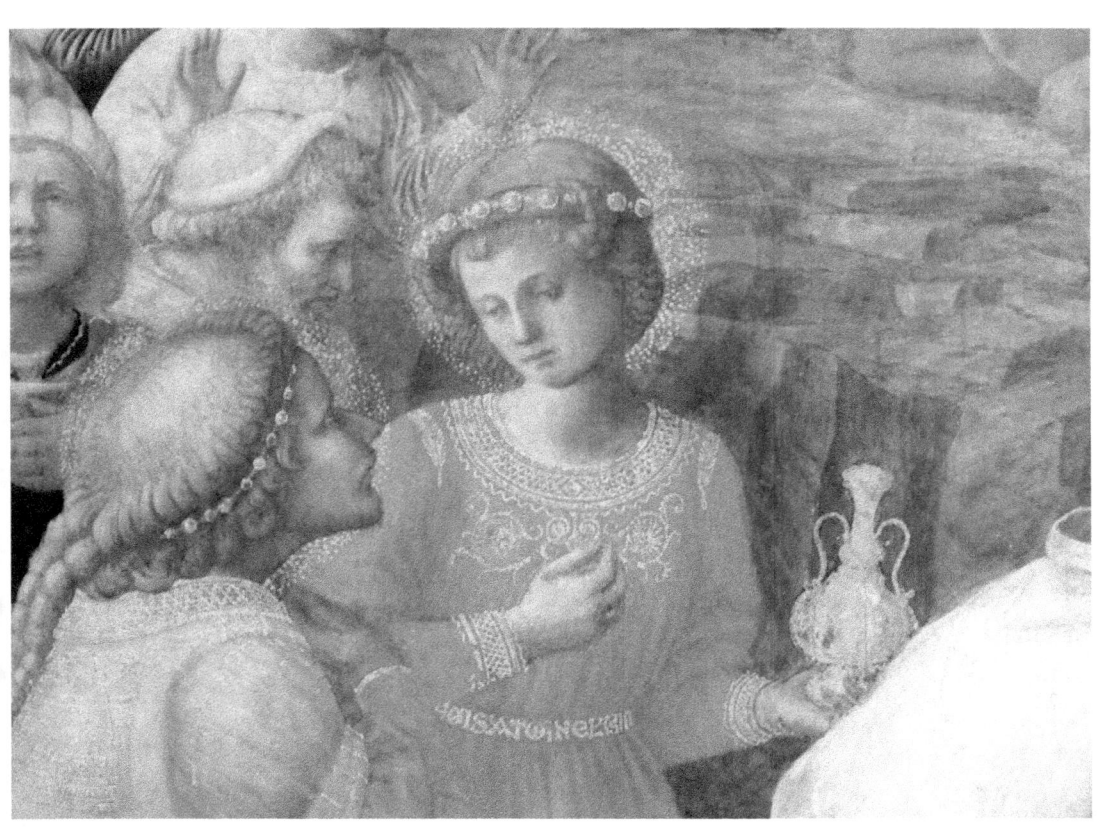

Fra Angelico, detail of Adoration of the Magi, 1445,
National Gallery of Art, Washington, DC (photo: author)

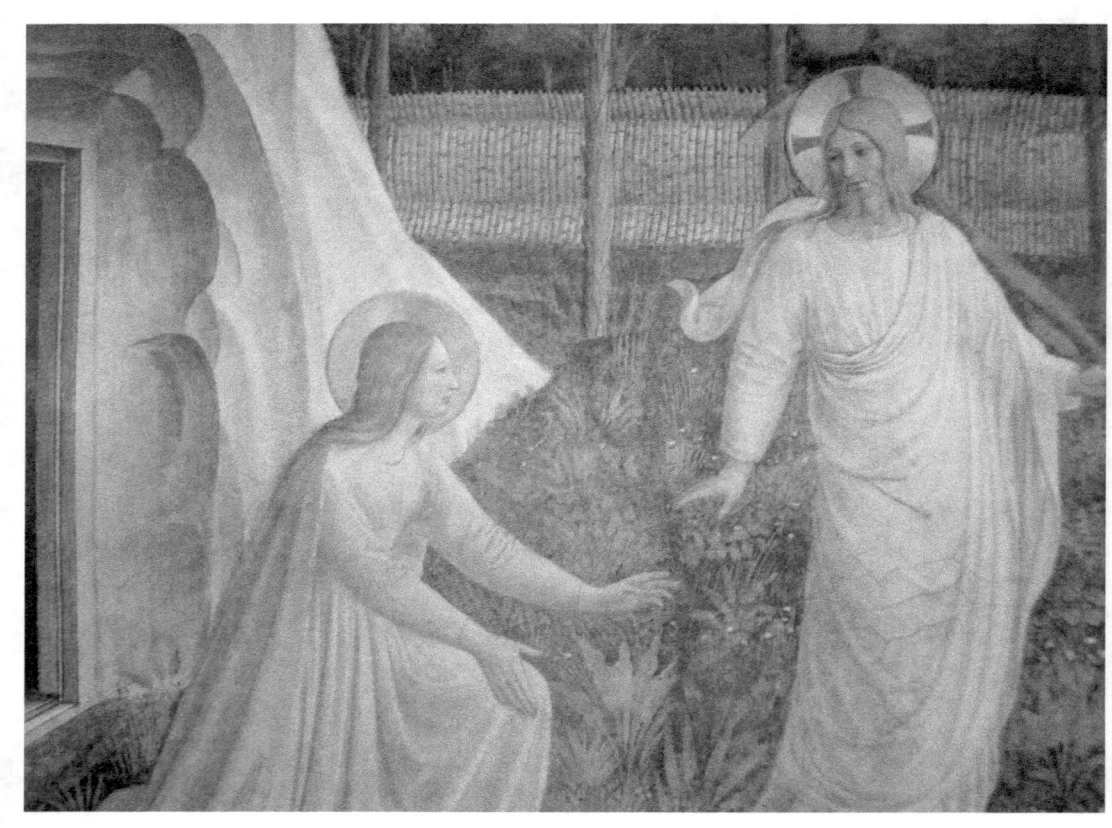

Fra Angelico, Noli Me Tangere

SUBJECTS FOR COMPOSITION AND SPECIAL TOPICS.

1. Angels in Art.
2. Savonarola, the Orator of San Marco.
3. Antonio, the Good Archbishop of Florence.
4. The Angel-Painter of San Marco.
5. An Illuminated Manuscript.
6. With Angelico on His Way to Rome.
7. In the Cells of San Marco.
8. How Monasteries Have Served Civilization.
9. A Day with the Dominicans at Fiesole.
10. Some Hill Towns of Tuscany.
11. Two Gothic Cathedrals of Italy. (Siena and Orvieto,)

REFERENCES FOR FRA ANGELICO.

1. Life of Fra Angelico *Sweetser*.
2. Life of Fra Angelico *Phillimor*.
3. Makers of Florence *Oliphant*.
4. Sketches and Studios in Southern Europe. (Orvieto) *Symonds*.
5. The Fine Arts *Symonds*.
6. Old Italian Masters *Cole*.
7. Friar Jerome's Beautiful Book *Aldrich*.
8. Art and Artists *Clement*.
9. Angels in Art *Clement*.
10. The Monk as Civilizer *Kingsley*.

Illustrations of art by contemporaries of Fra Angelico on the following pages.

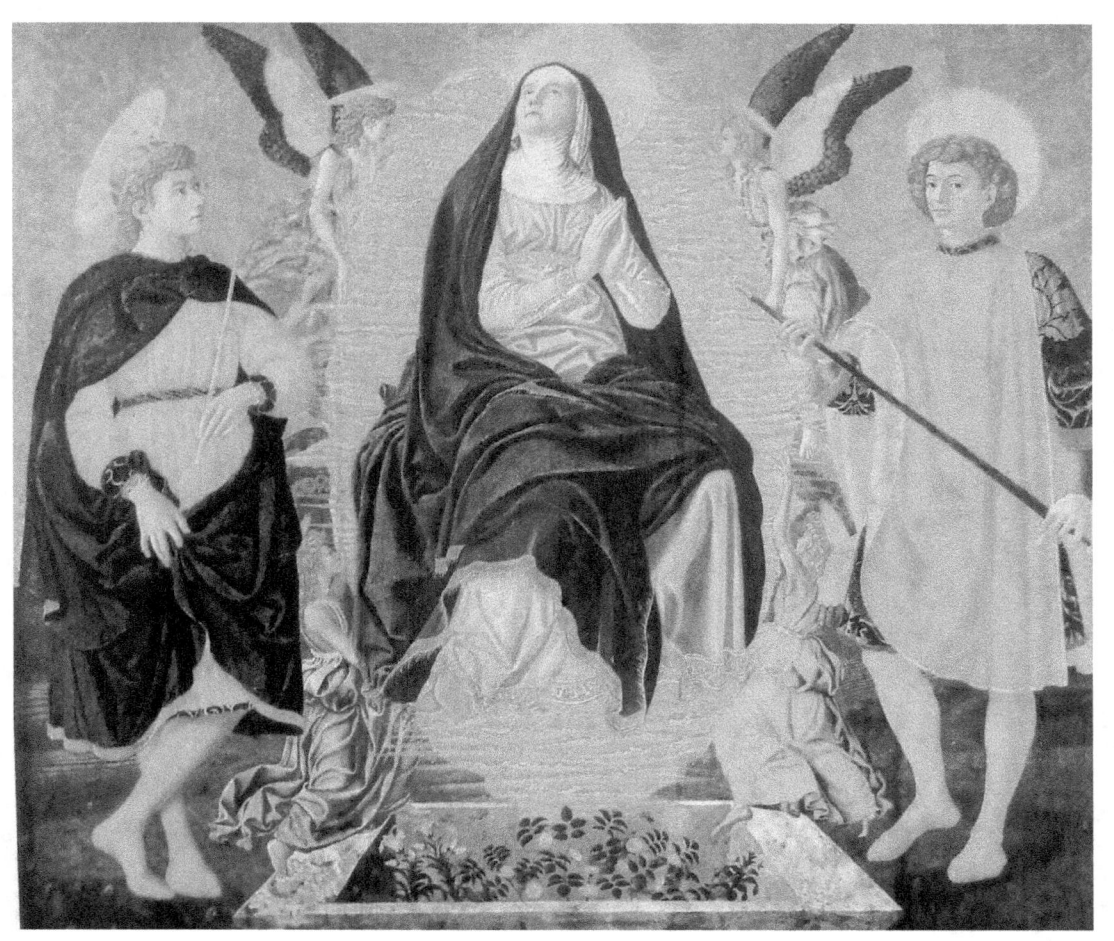

Andrea del Castagno, Assumption, Berlin

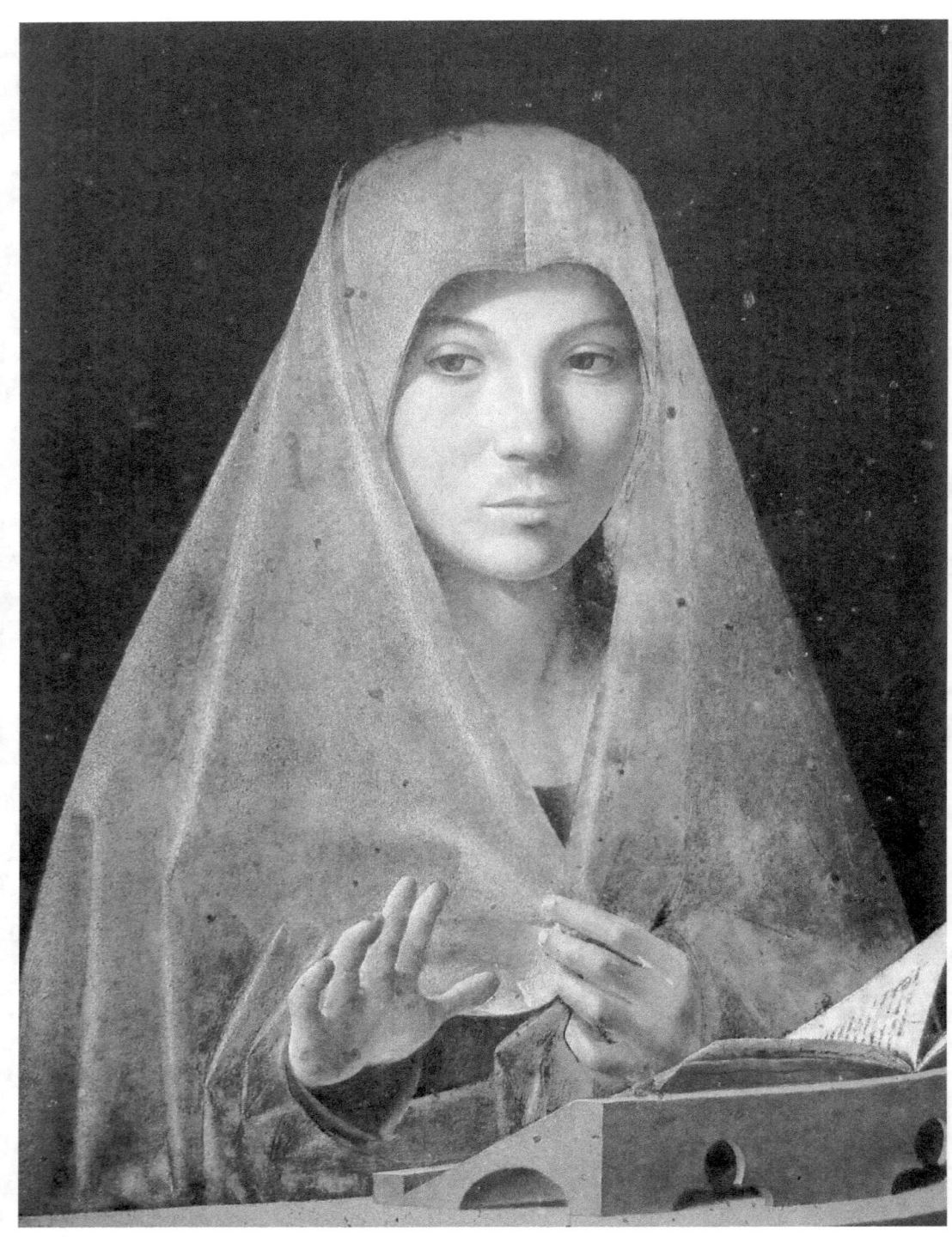

Antonello da Messina, The Virgin of the Annunciation, 1475, Palermo

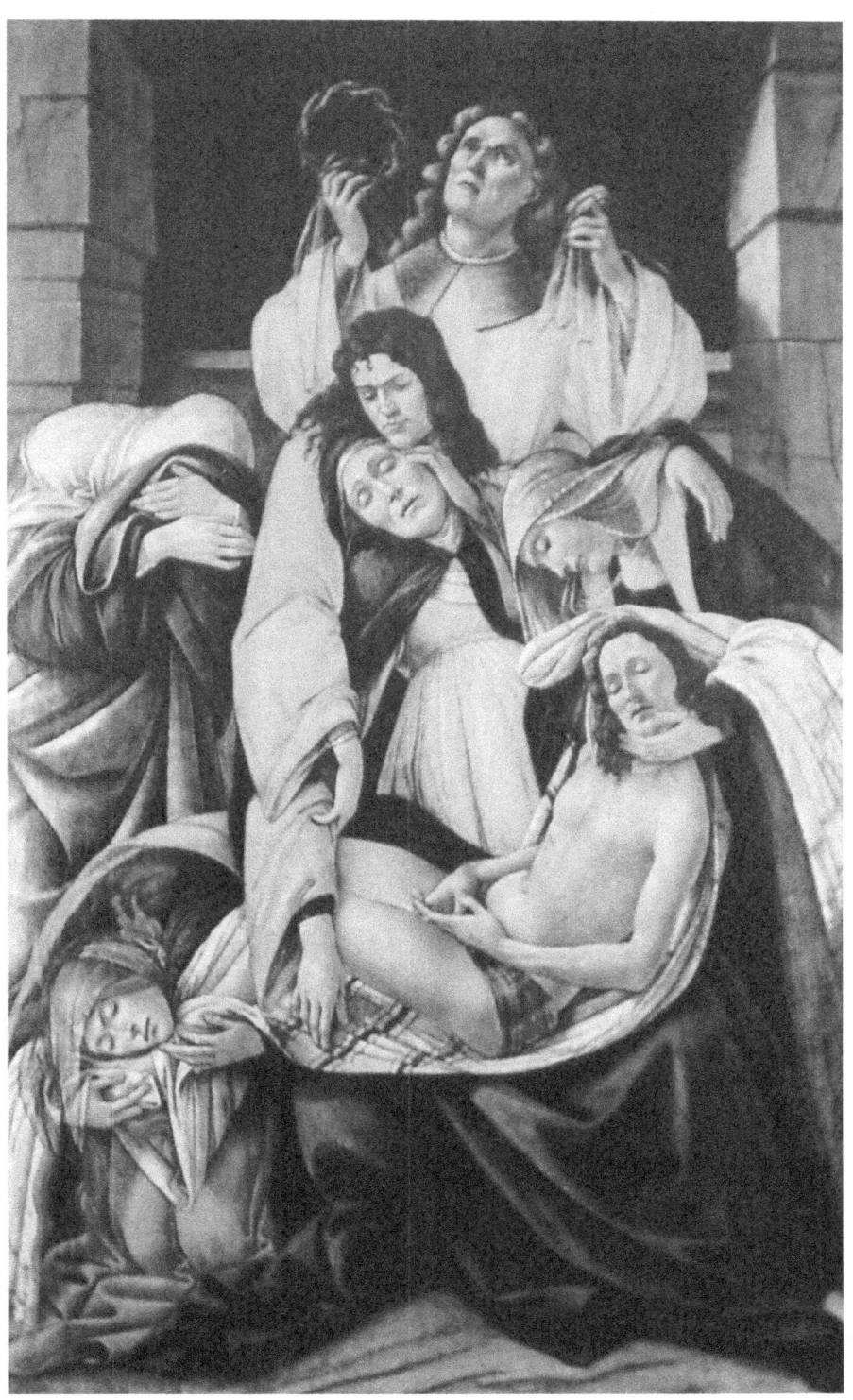

Sandro Botticelli, *Pietà*, Museo Poldi Pezzoli, Milan

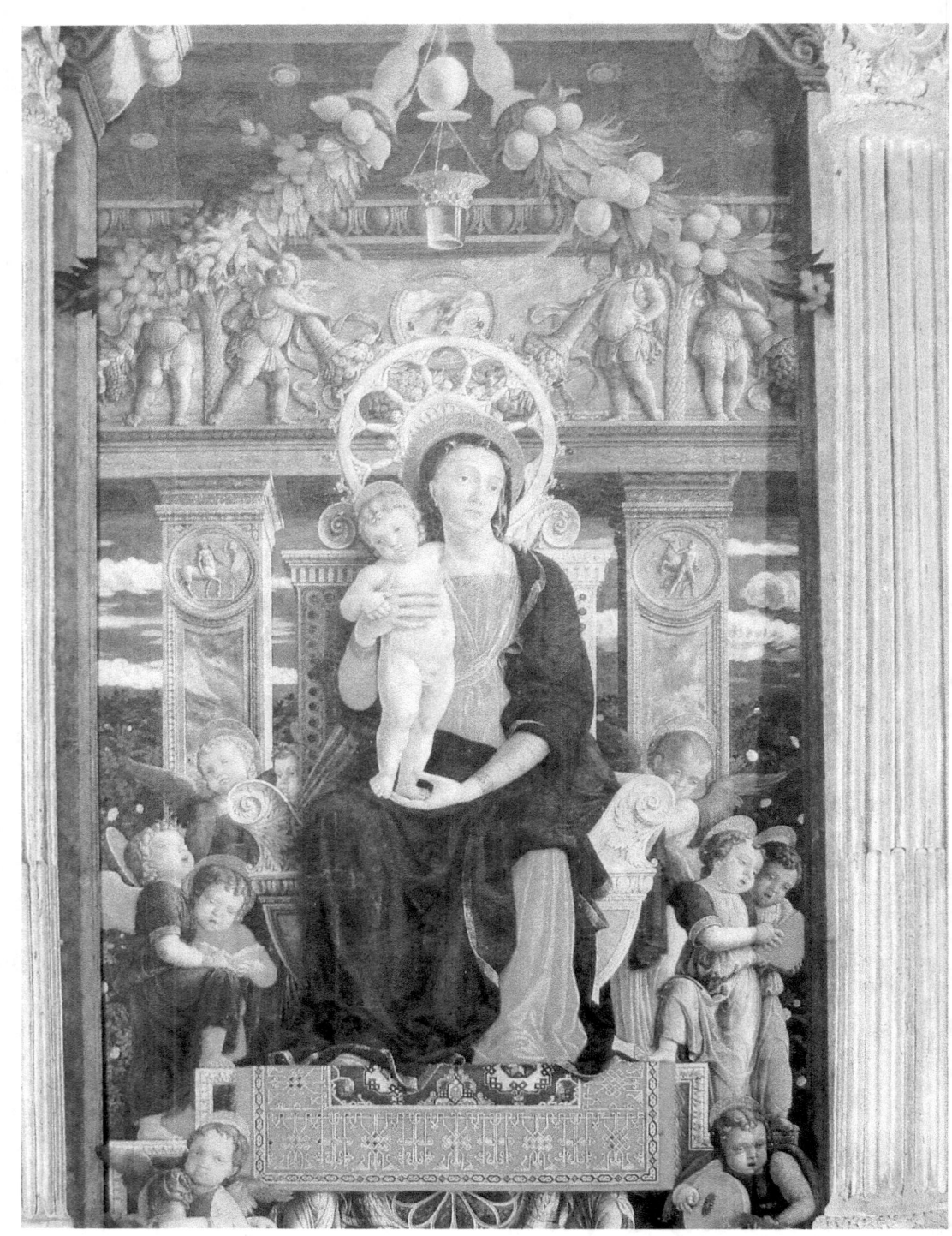

Andreas Mantegna, Madonna and Child Enthroned, 1457-60, Verona

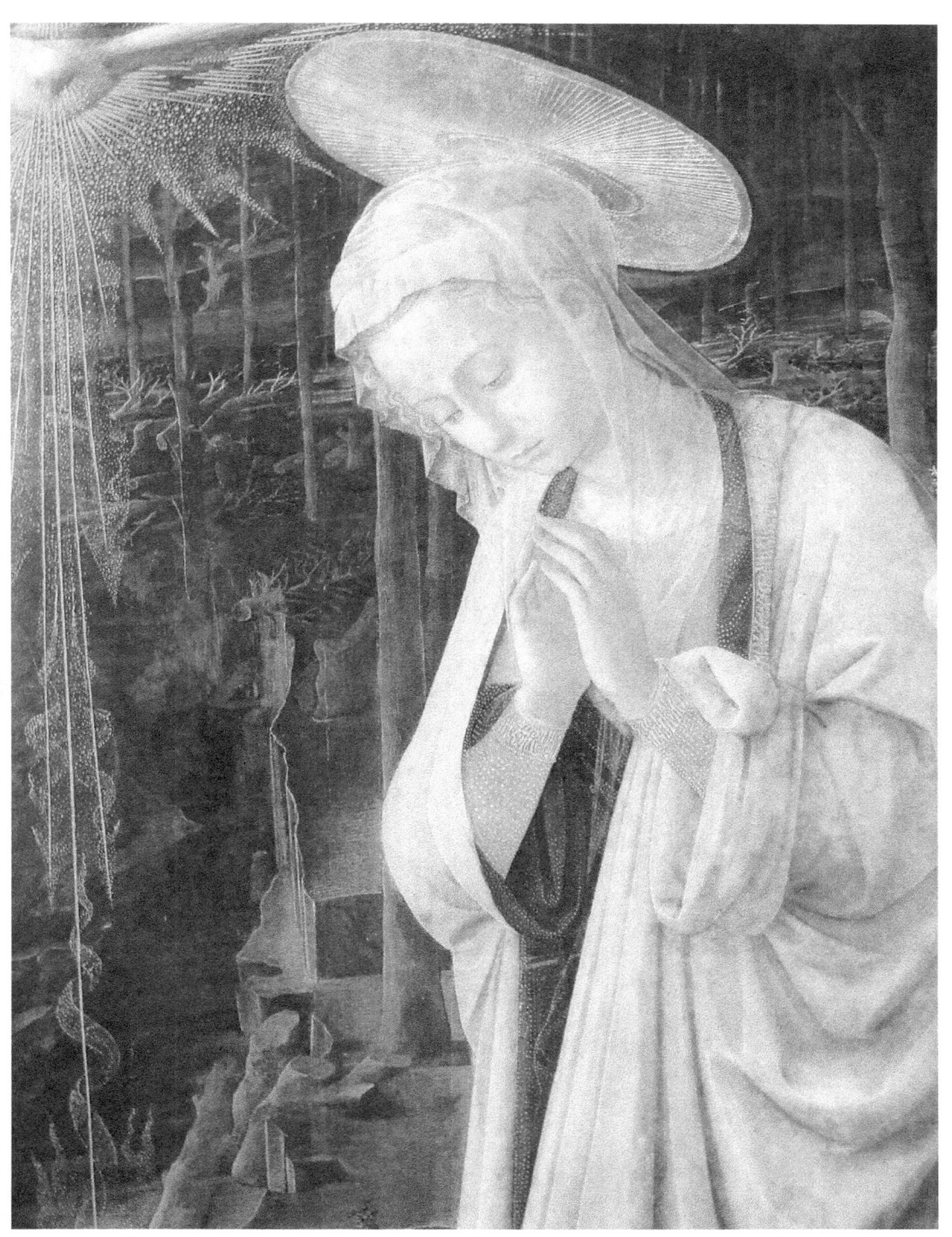

Fra Filippo Lippi, The Adoration of the Virgin, Berlin, detail

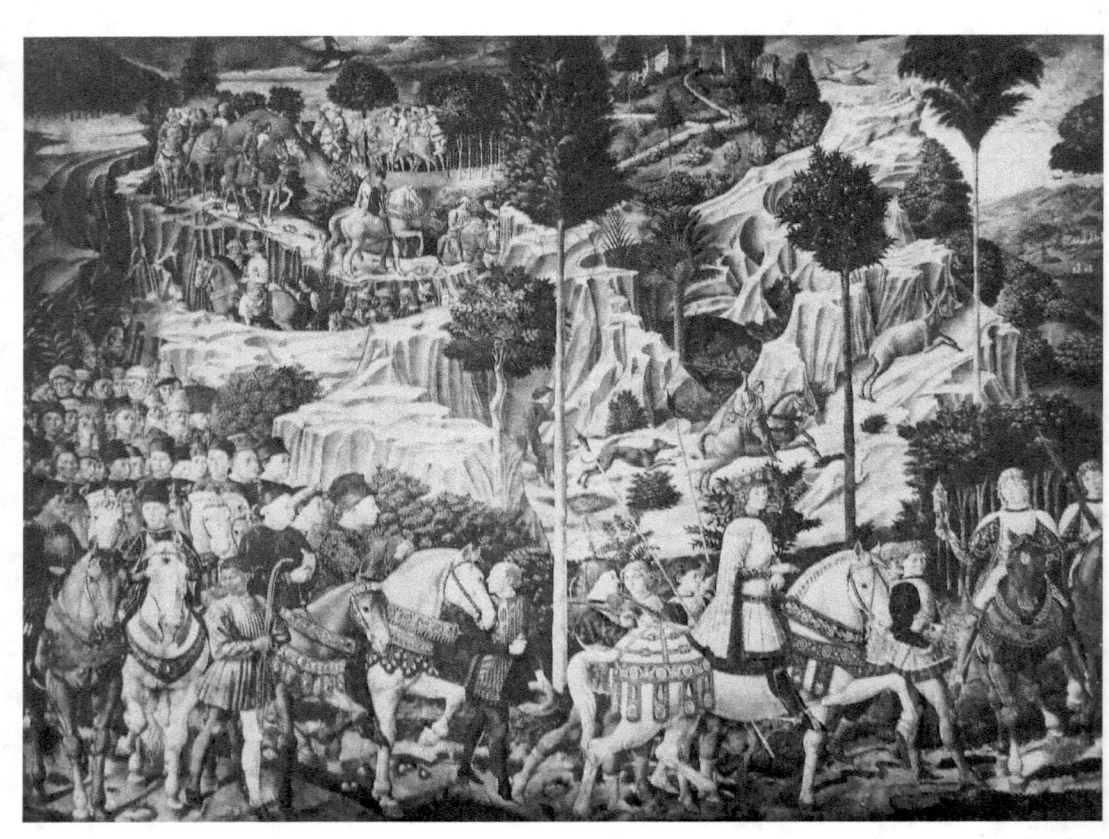

Benozzo Gozzoli, Journey of the Magi

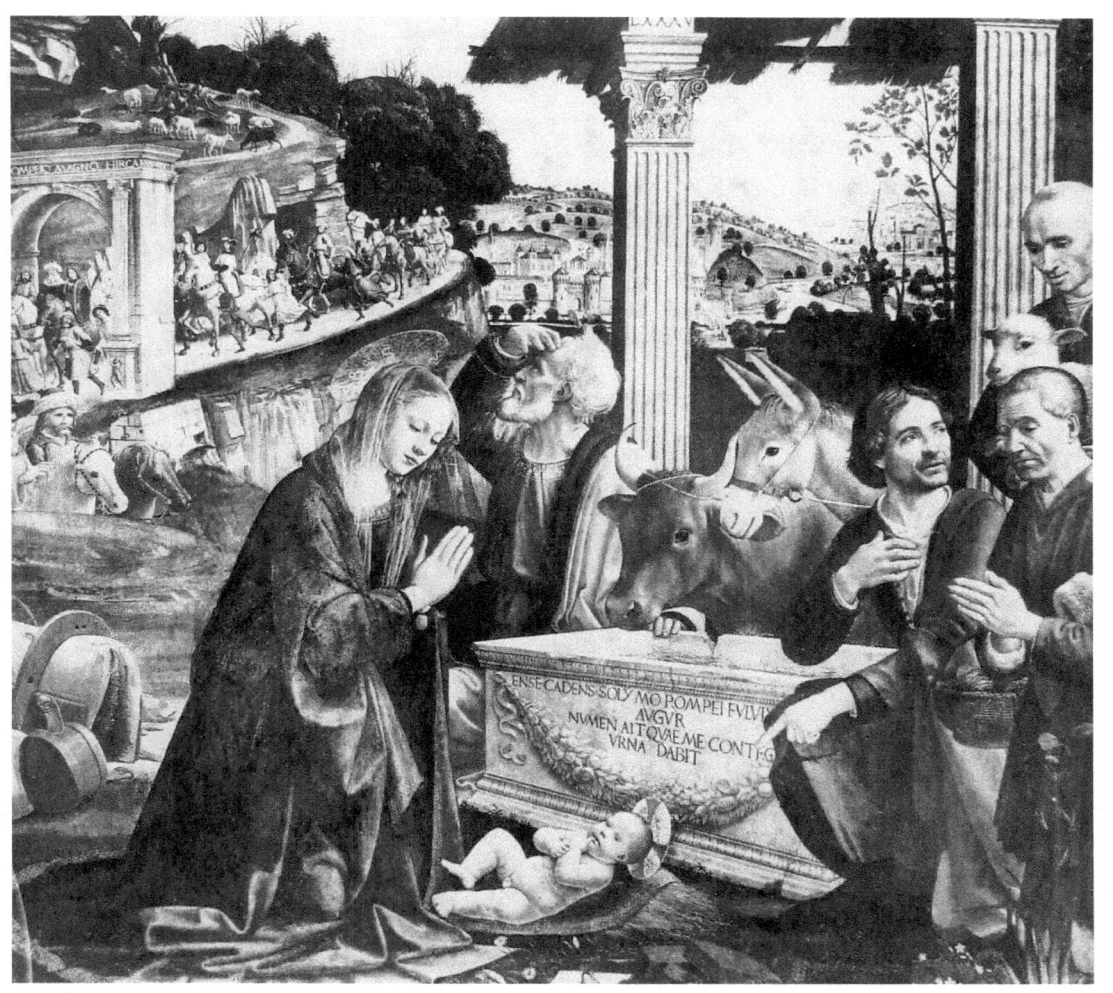

Domenico Ghirlandaio, Adoration of the Shepherds, 1485

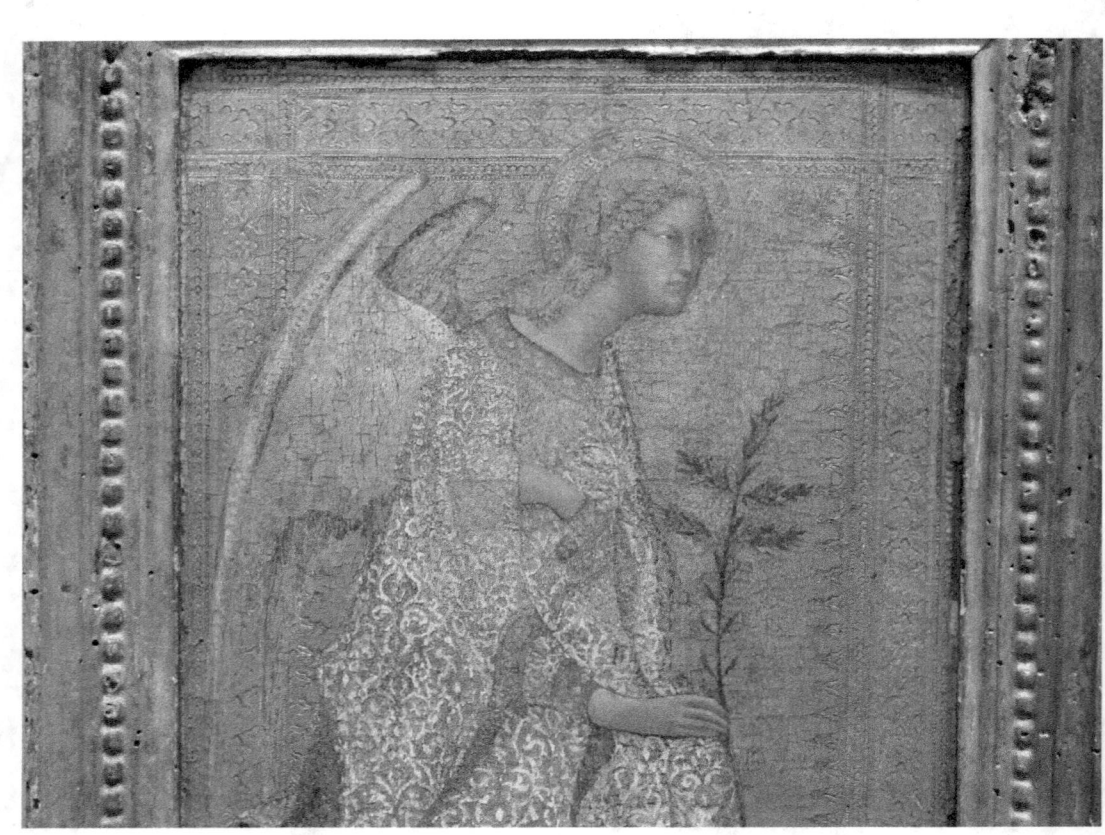

Simone Martini, Annunciation, Metropolitan Museum of Art, New York

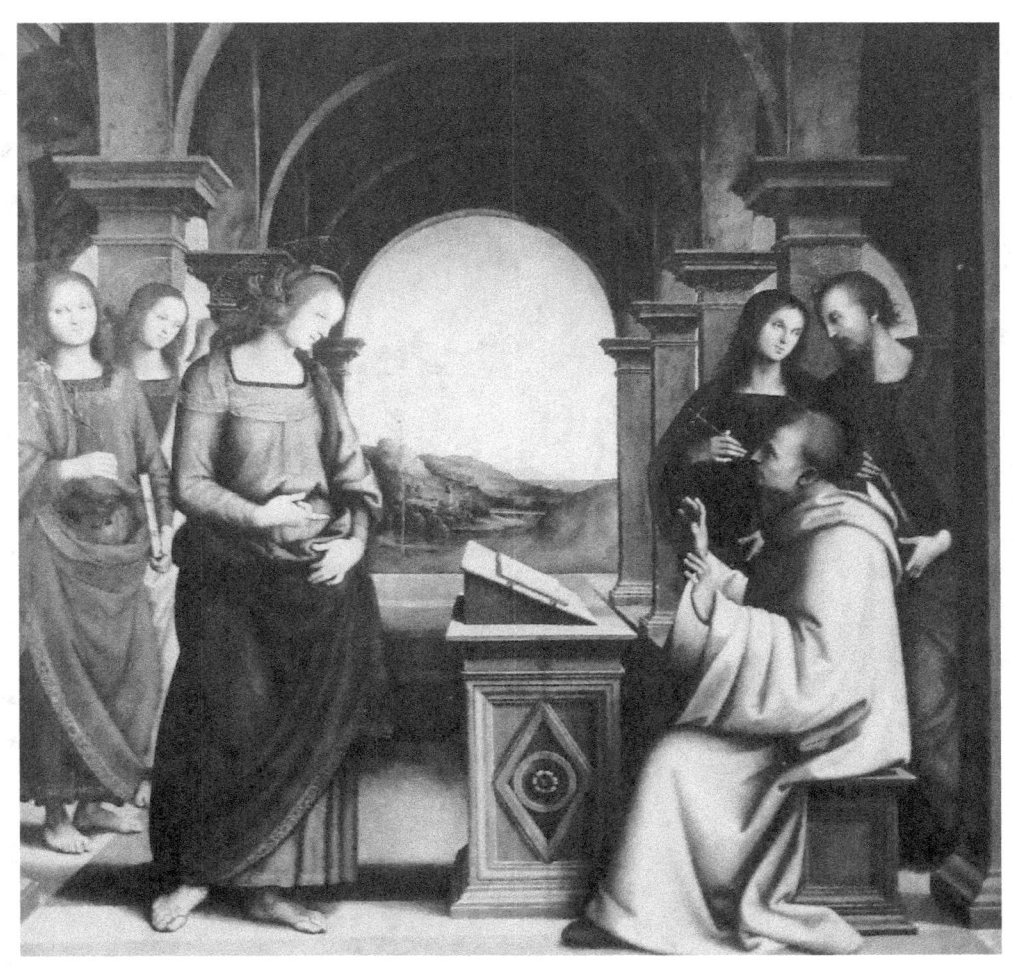

Perugino, Vision of St Bernard, 1488

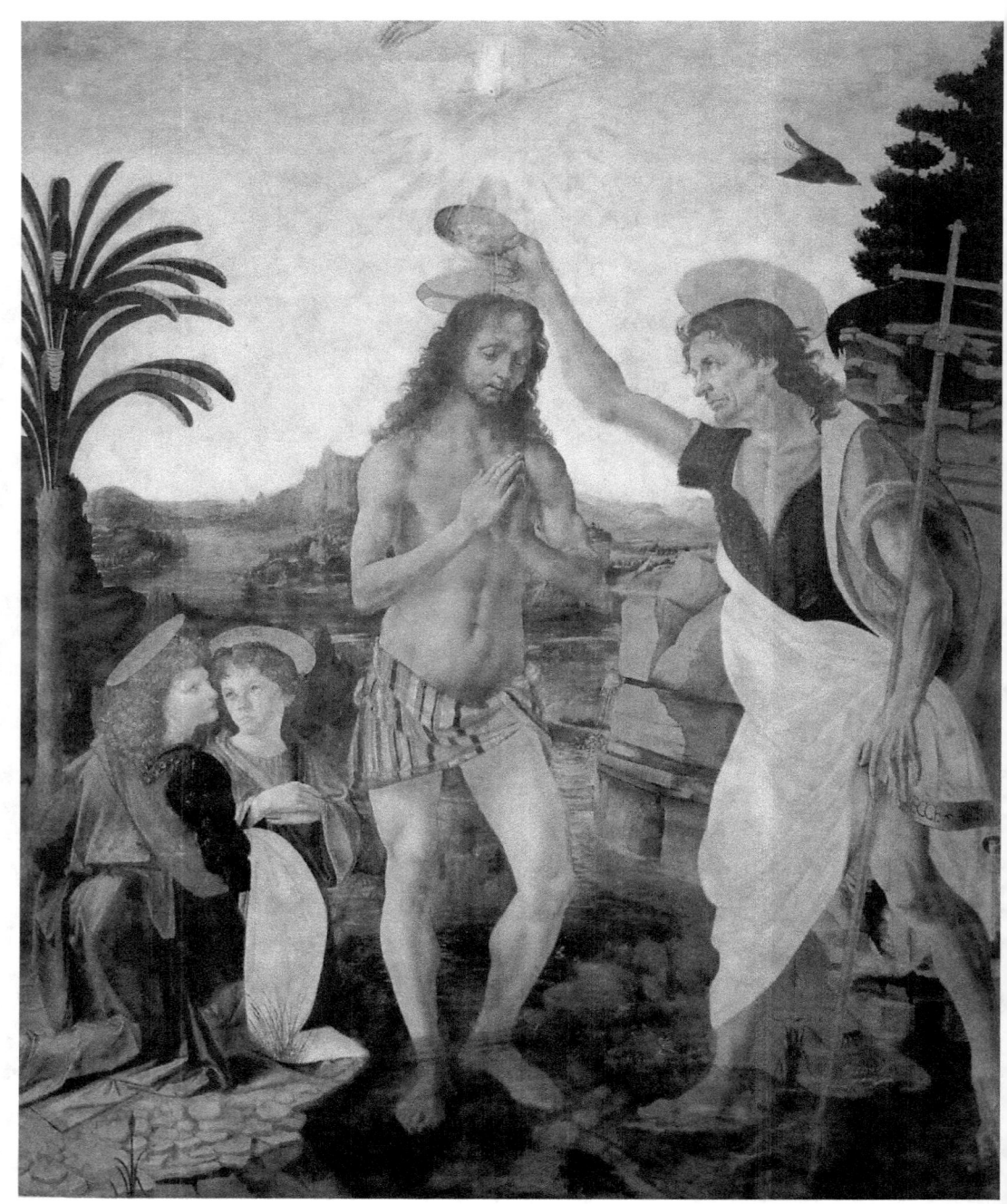

Andrea del Verrocchio, The Baptism of Christ

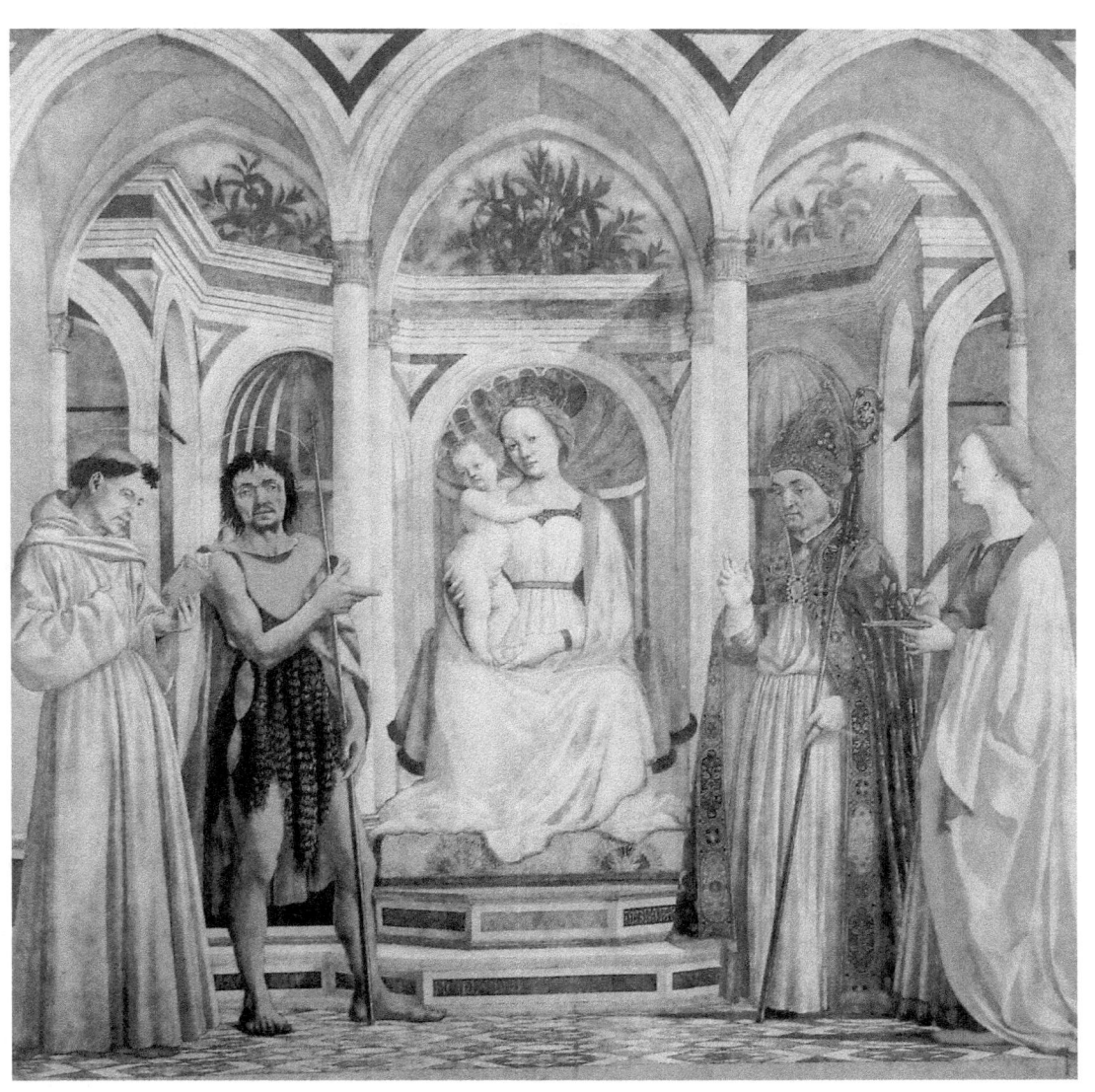

Domenico Veneziano, Madonna and Child With Saints, 1445, Uffizi Gallery

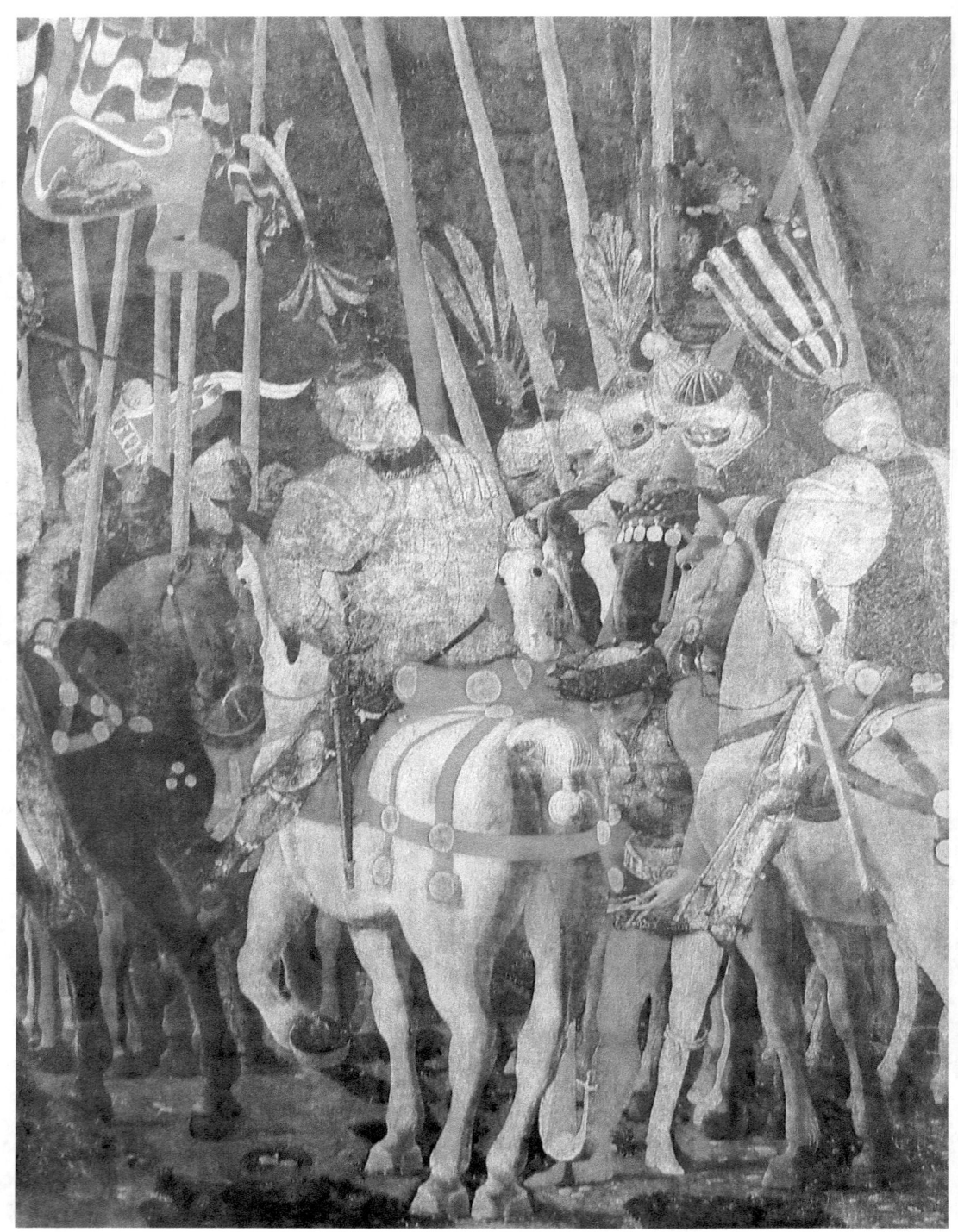

Paolo Uccello, Battle of San Romano, 1456-60, Loure, Paris

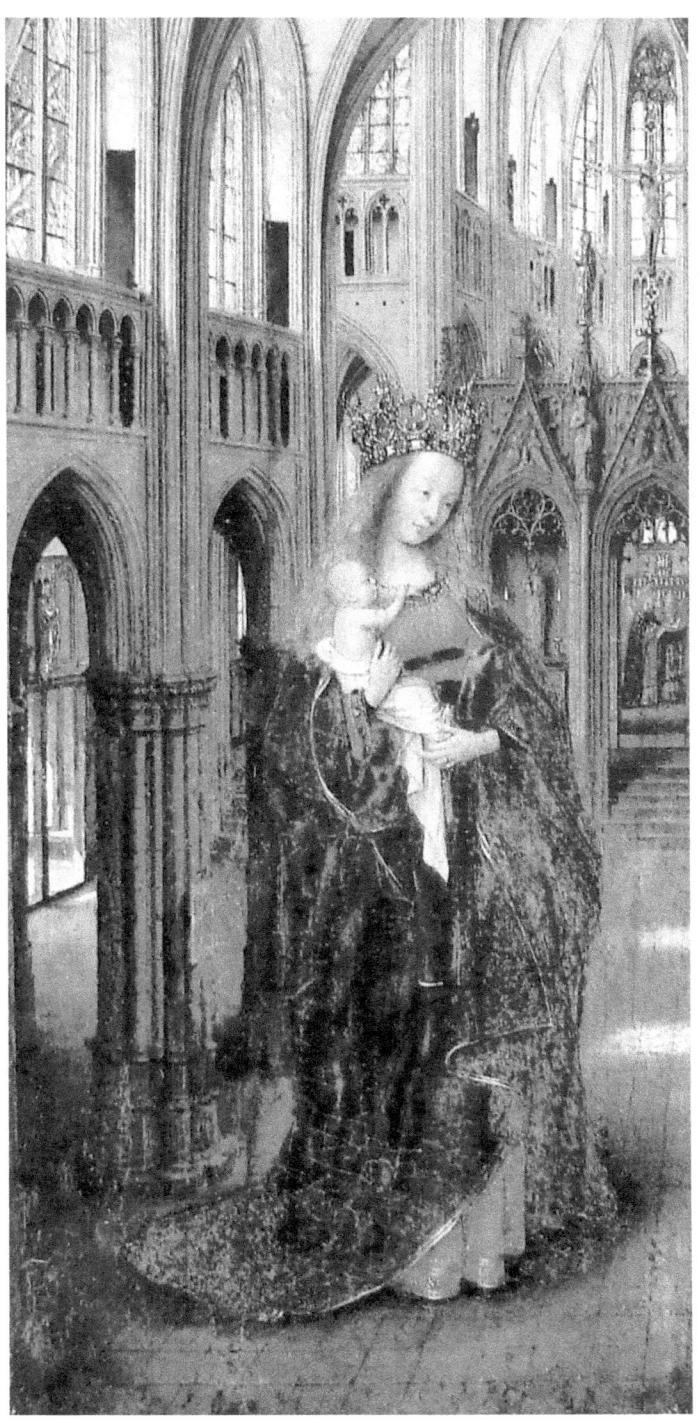

Jan van Eyck, Madonna In a Church, Berlin

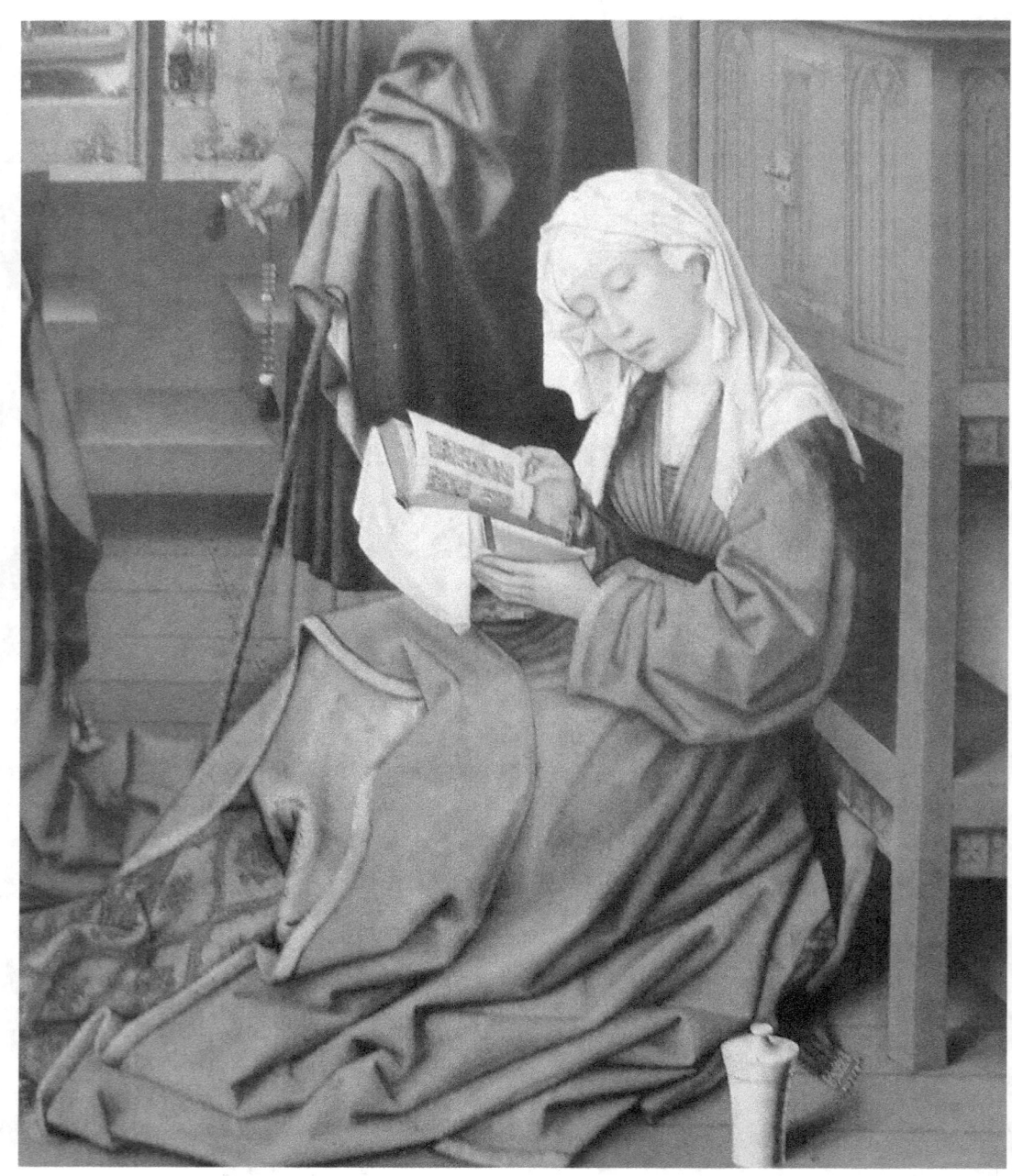

Rogier van der Weyden, Mary Magdalene Reading, detail, National Gallery, London

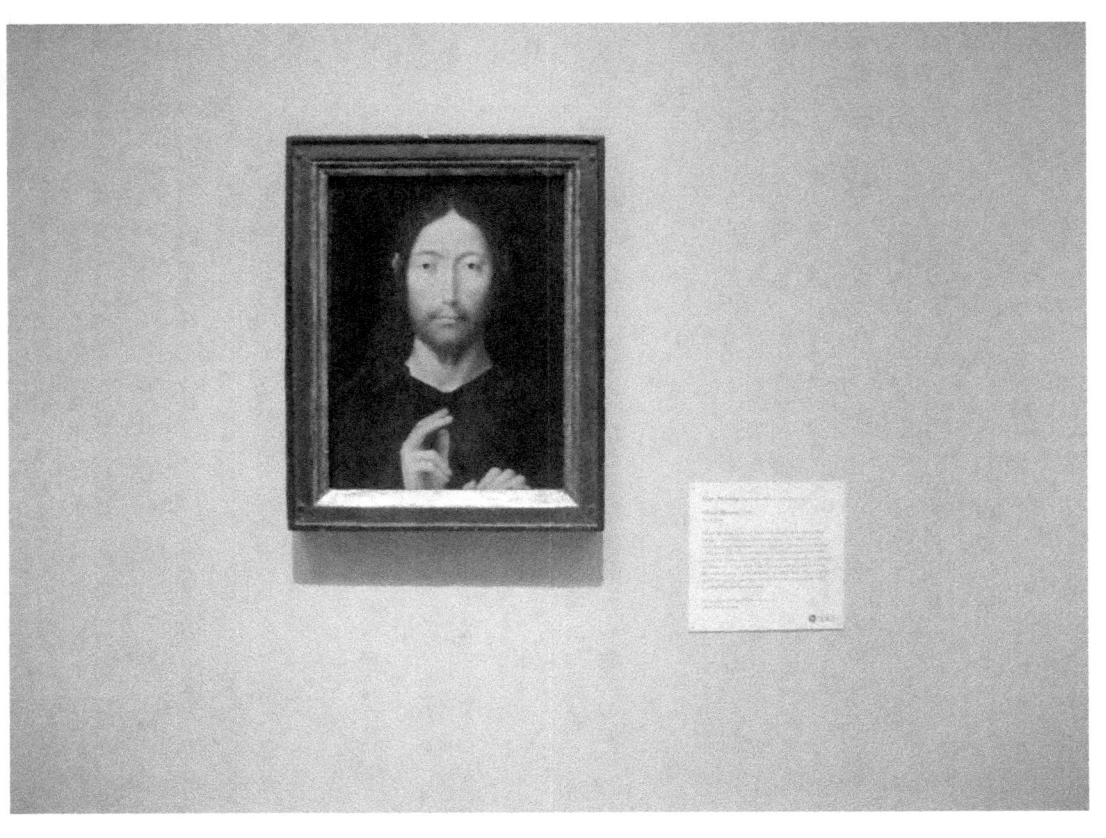

Hans Memling, Christ Blessing, Metropolitan Museum of Art

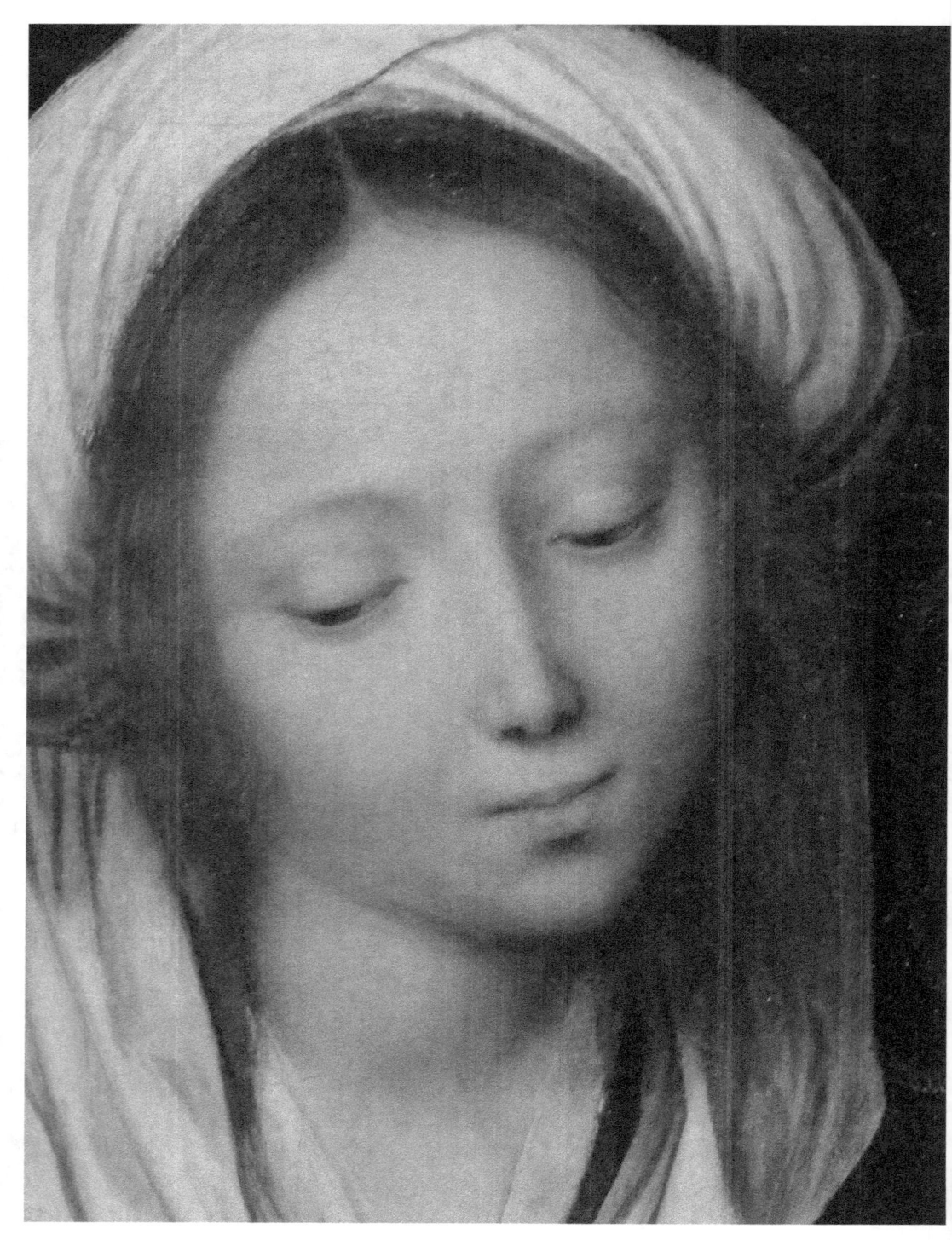

Gerard David, detail of the Adoration, Metropolitan Museum of Art

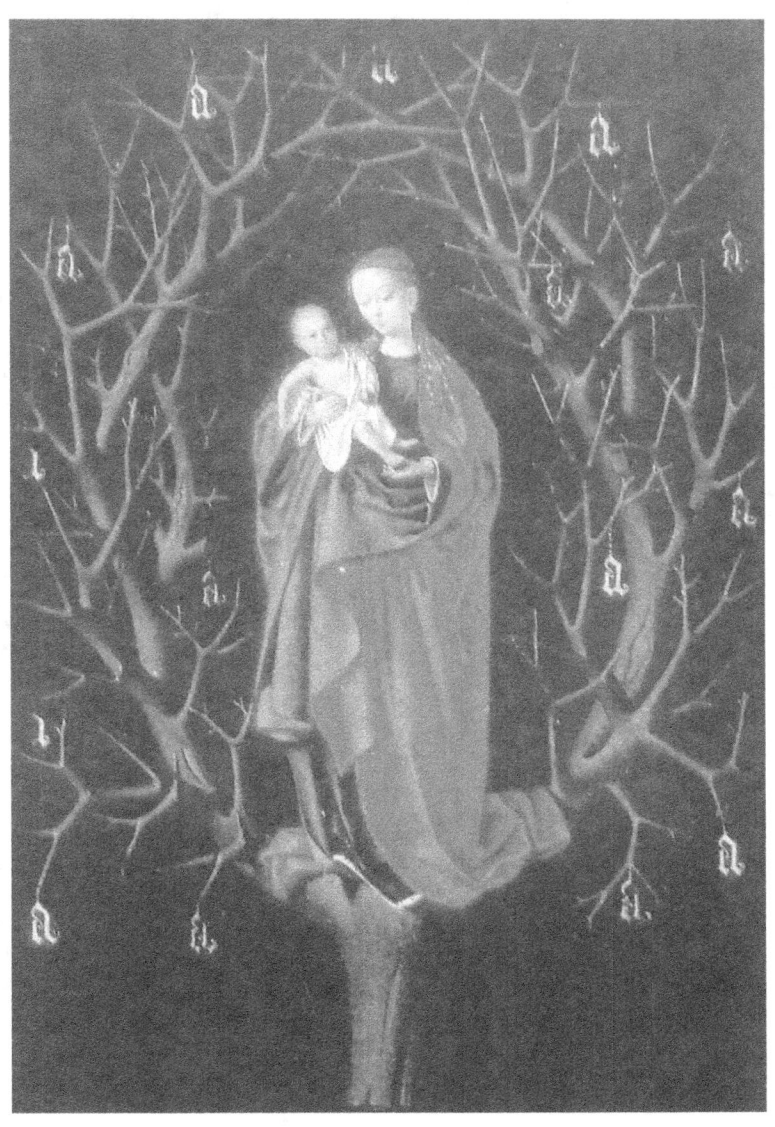

Petrus Christus, Madonna In a Barren Tree, 1450,
Prado, Madrid

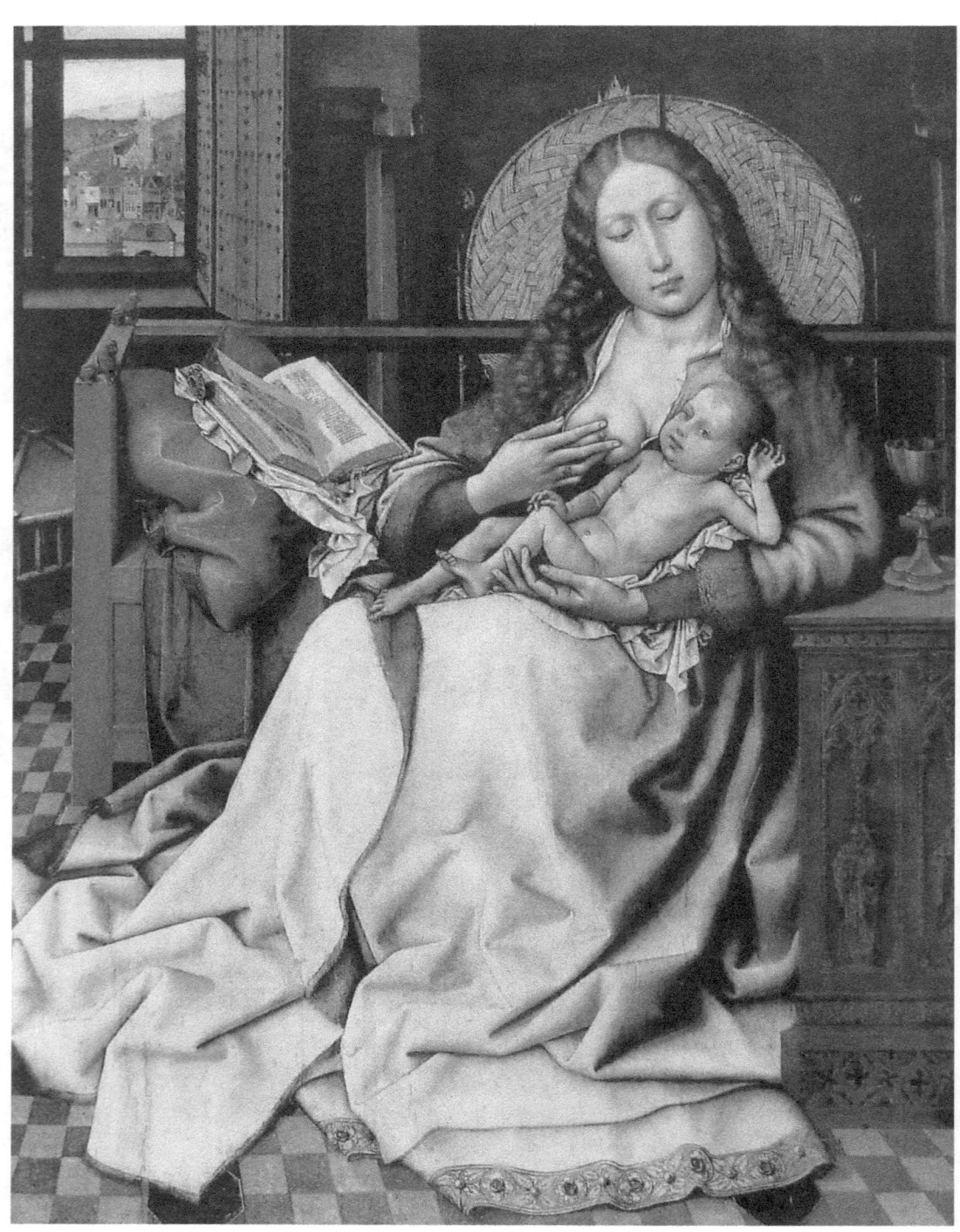

Robert Campin, Madonna With the Firescreen, National Gallery, London

BIBLIOGRAPHY[1]

I   *Fra Angelico*

C. Argan: *Fra Angelico*, Skira, Geneva 1955

U. Baldini: *Beato Angelico*, Edizioni d'Arte il Fiorino, Florence 1986

L. Berti et al: *Angelico at San Marco*, Sansoni, Florence 1965

M. OskovitsL "La fase tarda del Beato Angelico", *Arte cristiana*, LXXI, 1983, 11-24

— "Arte e formazione religosa – Il caso del Beato Angelico", in *L'uomo di fronte all'arte. Valori estetici e valori etico-religiosi*, La Spezia, 1985, *Vita e Pensiero*, 1986, 153-164

P. Cardile: "Fra Angelico's Shop at San Domenico in Fiesole", Ph. D thesis, Yale University 1974

G. Didi-Huberman: *Fra Angelico. Dissemblance et Figuration*, Flammarion, Paris 1990

— "La dissemblance des figures selon Fra Angelico", *Mélanges de l'Ecole Française de Rome. Moyn Age – Temps Moderne*, XCVIII, 1986, 709-802

D. Dini & G. Bonsanti: "Fra Angelico e gli affreschi nel Convento di San Marco (ca. 1441-50)", in E. Borsook & F. Superbi Gioffredi, ed: *Tecnica e Stile. Esempi di pittura murale del Rinascimento italiano*, Harvard Center for Italian Renaissance Studies at Villa I Tatti, 1986, 17-24

A. Francini Ciaranfi: *Beato Angelico: Gli affreschi di San Marco*, Amilcare Pizzi S. p. A, Milan 1940

C. Gilbert: "A Sign about Signing in a Fresco by Fra Angelico", in *Tribute to Lotte Brand Phi;lip*, Abaris Books, New York 1985, 65-70

— "Fra Angeloc", *Theologische Realenzyklopädie*, II, 5, Waler de Gruyter, Berlin, 19978, 710-3

---

1 From *Fra Angelico* by Rosalind Mutter, Crescent Moon, 2008.

—"The Conversion of Fra Angelico", in *Scritti di Storia dell'Arte in onore di Roberto Salvini*, ed. C. De Benedictis, G.C. Sansoni Editore Nuova, Florence 1984, 281-7

A. Hertz: *Fra Angelico*, Edizioni Paoline, Rome 1983

William Hood: *Fra Angelico at San Marco*, Yale University Press, New Haven 1993

—"Fra Angelico at San Marco: Art and the Liturgy of Cloistered Life", in T. Verdon & J. Henderson, eds: *Christianity and the Renaissance*, Syracuse University Press, Syracuse 1990, 108-131

—"St Dominic's Manners of Praying: Gestures in Fra Angelico's Frescoes at S. Marco", *Art bulletin*, LXVIII, 1986, 195-206

P. Joannides: "Fra Angelico: Two Annunciations", *Arte cristiana*, LXXVII, 1989, 303-308

R. Krautheimer: "Fra Angelico and – perhaps – Alberti", in J. Plummer & I. Lavin, eds: *Studies in Late Medieval and Renaissance Painting Presented to Millard Meiss*, New York University Press, New York 1977, 290-296

A. Ladis: "Fra Angelico: newly discovered document from the 1420s", *Mitteilungen des Kunsthistorischen Institutes in Florenz*, XXV, 1981, 378-9

Christopher Lloyd: *Fra Angelico*, Phaidon 1979

S. Madigan: "A New Interpretation of the Iconography of Fra Angelico: Rosarian Organization in the Frescoed Cells of San Marco", MACAA paper, Hamlite University, St Paul, 1977

J. Miller: "Medici Patronage and the Iconography of Fra Angelico's San Marco Altarpiece", *Studies in Iconography*, XI, 1987, 1-13

S. Orlandi: *Beato Angelico*, Leo S. Olscki, Florence 1964

John Pope-Hennessy: *Fra Angelico*, Phaidon 1974

U. Procacci: "Recent restoration in Florence, II: Fra Angelico, Sassetta and others", *Burlington Magazine*, LXXXIX, 1947, 330-4

M. Salmi: *Beato Angelico*, Edizioni Valori Plastici, Rome 1958

P. Sheaffer: "White Light and Meditation at San Marco", *Memorie Domenicane*, XIV, 1983, 329-334

I. Strunk: *Fra Angelico aus dem Dominikanerorden*, B. Kuehlens Kunstanstalt u. Verlag, Gladbach 1916

C.G. Argan: *The Renaissance*, Thames & Hudson 1969

Karen Armstrong: *The Gospel According to Woman; Christianity's Creation of the Sex War in the West*, Pan 1987

Karen Arthurs: *A Survey of the Notions Behind, and the Mechanics of, Harmony Within the Composition of Art From Prehistory to the Renaissance*, BA thesis, Newcastle Polytechnic 1984

Geoffrey Ashe: *The Virgin: Mary's Cult and the Re-emergence of the Goddess*, Arkana 1987

—*Discovering the Goddess: A Personal Testimony*, Crescent Moon 1995

Michael Baxandall: *Painting and Experience in 15th Century Italy*, Oxford University Press 1988

—*Patterns of Intention: On the Historical Explanation of Pictures*, Yale University Press 1985

James Beck: *Italian Renaissance Painting*, Harper & Row, New York 1981

Ean Begg: *The Cult of the Black Virgin*, Routledge 1985

Bernard Berenson: *The Italian Painters of the Renaissance*, Phaidon 1952

—*Looking at Pictures with Bernard Berenson*, selected by Hann Kiel, Abrahams, New York 1974

Pamela Berger: *The Goddess Obscured*, Robert Hale 1988

Bruce Bernard: *The Queen of Heaven: A Selection of Painting the Virgin from the Twelfth to the Eighteenth Centuries*, Macdonald/ Orbis 1987

—*The Bible and Its Painters*, Orbis 1983

Botticelli: *The Complete Paintings of Botticelli*, Granada 1980

Charles Bouleau: *The Painter's Secret Geometry: A Study of Composition in Art*, tr Jonathan Griffin, Thames & Hudson 1963

Serge Bramly: *Leonardo: The Artist and the Man*, Michael Joseph 1992

Allan Brahama: *Italian Renaissance Painters of the Sixteenth Century*, National Gallery 1985

Helmut Brinker: *Zen in the Art of Painting*, Routledge & Kegan Paul 1987

Stephanie Brown: *Religious Painting*, Phaidon 1979

Jacob Burckhardt: *The Altarpiece in Renaissance Italy*, Phaidon 1988

Titus Burckhardt: *Sacred Art in East and West*, Perennial Book, Middlesex 1967

Ritchie Calder: *Leonardo and The Age of the Eye*, Heinemann 1970

Joseph Campbell: *The Power of Myth*, with Bill Moyers, ed. Betty Sue Flowers, Doubleday, New York 1988

Michael P. Carroll: *The Cult of the Virgin Mary*, Princeton University

Press, New Jersey 1986

Richard Cavendish: *Visions of Heaven and Hell*, Orbis 1977

Andre Chastel: *Art of the Italian Renaissance*, tr Peter & Linda Murray, Alpine Fine Arts Collection 1985

—*The Studios and Styles of the Renaissance, Italy 1460-1500*, tr Griffin, Thames & Hudson 1966

Herschel B. Chipp, ed. *Theories of Modern Art*, University Press of California, Los Angeles 1968

Bruce Cole: *The Renaissance Artist at Work*, John Murray 1983

Charles D. Cuttler: *Northern Painting From Pucelle to Bruegel*, Holt, Rineheart & Winston, New York 1968

Lene Dresen-Coenders, ed: *Saints and She-Devils: Images of Women in the 15th and 16th Centuries*, Rubicon Press 1987

Steven C. Dubin: *Arresting Images: Impolitic Art and Uncivil Actions*, Routledge 1992

Andrea Dworkin: *Intercourse*, Arrow 1988

—*Pornography: Men Possessing Women*, Women's Press 1984

Donald Ehresmann: "Some Observations on the Role of the Liturgy in the Early Winged Altarpiece", *Art Bulletin*, LXIV, 1982

Colin Eisler: *Early Netherlandish Painting: The Thyssen-Bornemisza Collection*, Sotheby's Publications 1989

Mircea Eliade: *Ordeal by Labyrinth*, University of Chicago Press 1984

—*Symbolism, the Sacred and the Arts*, Crossroad, New York 1985

Joan Evans, ed: *The Flowering of the Middle Ages*, Thames & Hudson 1966

Giorgio T. Faggin: *The Complete Paintings of the Van Eycks*, Wiedenfeld & Nicolson 1970

John Fletcher & Andrew Benjamin, ed; *Abjection, Melancholia and Love: the Work of Julia Kristeva*, Routledge 1990

S.J. Freedberg: *Painting of the High Renaissance in Rome and Florence*, Harper & Row, New York 1972

Sigmund Freud: *Leonardo da Vinci*, tr Alan Tyson, Penguin 1963

Max J. Friedlander: *From Van Eyck to Bruegel*, Phaidon 1969

—*The van Eycks, Petrus Christus*, Early Netherlandish Painting vol. 1, tr Heinz Norden, Sijthoff, Leyden, Netherlands 1967

Eugène Fromentin: *The Masters of Past Time: Dutch and Flemish Painting from Van Eyck to Rembrandt*, Phaidon 1981

Niny Garavaghlia: *The Complete Paintings of Mantegna*, Weidenfeld & Nicholson 1971

Fred Gettings: *The Hidden Art: A Study of the Occult Symbolism in Art*, Studio Vista 1978

Matila Ghyka: *The Geometry of Art and Life*, Sheed & Ward, New York

1946

Marija Gimbutas: *The Language of the Goddess*, Thames & Hudson 1989

Rona Goffen: *Giovanni Bellini*, Yale University Press, New Haven 1989

Robert Goldwater & Marco Treves, eds. *Artists on Art*, John Murray 1975

E.H. Gombrich: *Norm and Form: Studies in the Renaissance I*, Phaidon 1985

— *Symbolic Images, Renaissance Studies II*, Phaidon 1985

Cecil Gould: *Leonardo: The Artist and the Non-Artist*, Weidenfeld & Nicholson 1975

— "On the Direction of Light in Italian Renaissance Frescoes and Altarpieces", *Gazette des Beaux-Arts*, 6, XCVII, 1981

John Hale: *Italian Renaissance Painting*, Phaidon 1977

James Hall: *A Dictionary of Subjects and Symbols in Art*, John Murray 1984

Frederick Hartt: *History of Italian Renaissance Art: Painting, Sculpture, Architecture*, Thomas & Hudson 1987

— *Sandro Botticelli*, Collins 1954

P. Jolly: "Rogier van der Weyden's Escorial and Philadelphia *Crucifixions* and their relation to Fra Angelico at San Marco", *Oud Holland*, XCV, 1981, 113-126

Julia Kristeva: *The Kristeva Reader*, ed Toril Moi, Blackwell 1986

— *Desire in Language: A Semiotic Approach to Literature and Art*, ed Leon Roudiez, tr Thomas Gora, Alice Jardine & Leon Roudiez, Blackwell 1982

Weston La Barre: *The Ghost Dance*, Allen & Unwin 1972

Barbara Lane: *The Altar and the Altarpiece: Sacramental Themes in Early Netherlandish Painting*, New York 1984

— "Sacred vs Profane in Early Netherlandish Painting", *Simiolus*, XVIII, 1988

Leonardo da Vinci: *The Drawings of Leonardo da Vinci*, introduction A.E. Popham, Cape, 1964

— *Selections from the Notebooks*, Oxford University Press 1952

Michael Levey: *High Renaissance*, Penguin 1975

— *Early Renaissance*, Penguin 1967

Robert Longhi: *Piero della Francesca*, Milan 1955

Emile Male: *The Gothic Image*, Collins 1961

Elaine Marks & Isabelle de Courtivron, eds: *New French Feminisms: an Anthology*, Harvester Wheatsheaf 1981

G. Marchini: *Filippo Lippi*, Electa Editrice, Milan 1975

James Marrow: "Symbol and Meaning in Northern European Art of the Late Middle Ages and Early Renaissance", *Simiolus*, XVI, 1986

Milliard Meiss: "Light as Form and Symbol in Some Fifteenth Century Paintings", *Art Bulletin*, XXVII, 1945

J.C.J. Metford: *Dictionary of Christian Lore and Legend*, Thames & Hudson 1983

Edward Mullins: *The Painted Witch: Female Body, Male Art*, Secker & Warburg 1985

Peter & Linda Murray: *The Penguin Dictionary of Art and Artists*, Penguin 1976

Linda Murray: *High Renaissance*, Thames & Hudson 1977

Lynda Nead: *Female Nude: Art, Obscenity and Sexuality*, Routledge 1992

Erich Neumann: *The Great Mother*, Princeton University Press, New Jersey 1972

Shirley Nicholson, ed. *The Goddess Re-awakening: The Goddess Principle Today* Theosophical Publishing House, New York 1989

Rudolf Otto: *The Idea of the Holy*, Oxford University Press 1958

Erwin Panofsky: *Studies in Iconology*, Harper & Row, New York 1972
— *Early Netherlandish Painting*, Harvard University Press, Mass., 1953

Walter Pater: *The Renaissance*, Oxford University Press 1980

Michael Payne: *Reading Theory: An Introduction to Lacan, Derrida, and Kristeva*, Blackwell 1993

Robert Payne: *Leonardo da Vinci*, Robert hale 1979

Lotte Brand Philip: *The Ghent Altarpiece and the Art of Jan van Eyck*, Princeton University Press 1971

C. Purtle: *The Marian Paintings of Jan van Eyck*, Princeton University Press, Princeton 1982

Kathleen J. Reiger, ed: *The Spiritual Image in Modern Art,* Theosophical Publ-ishing House, Wheaton, Illinois 1987

D. Robb: "The Iconography of the Annunciation in the Fourteenth and Fifteenth Centuries", *Art Bulletin*, XVIII, 1936, 480-526

John Ruskin: *Works*, ed. E.T.Cook & A. Wedderburn, 39 vols, Allen 1903-12

Monica Sjöo & Barbara Mor: *The Great Cosmic Mother*, Harper & Row, San Francisco 1987

Alistair Smith: *Early Netherlandish and German Painting*, National Gallery 1985

J. Spencer: "Spatial Imagery of the Annunciation in Fifteenth-century Florence", *Art Bulletin*, XXXVI, 1955, 273-280

Oswald Spengler: *The Decline of the West*, Allen & Unwin 1961

Wolfgang Stechow: *Northern Renaissance Art, 1400-1600, Sources and Documents*, Prentice-Hall, New Jersey 1966

L. Steinberg & S. Edgerton: "How shall this be? Reflections on Filippo Lippi's *Annunciation* in London", *Artibus et Historiæ*, VIII, 1987, 25-53

Victor I. Stoichita: *Leonardo da Vinci*, Abbey Library 1978

Nicholas Usherwood: *The Bible in 20th Century Art*, Pagoda Books 1987

Lionello Venturi: *Renaissance Painting, from Leonardo to Dürer*, Skira/ Macmillan 1979

— *Italian Paintings*, Zwemmer 1950

— *Botticelli*, Phaidon 1964

Marina Warner: *Alone Of All Her Sex: The Myth and Cult of the Virgin Mary*, Picador 1985

— *Monuments and Maidens*, Weidenfeld & Nicholson 1985

Margaret Whinney: *Early Flemish Painters*, Faber 1966

John White: *The Birth and Rebirth of Pictorial Space*, Faber 1957/87

Peter Lamborn Wilson: *Angels*, Thames & Hudson 1980

Heinrich Wolfflin: *Classic Art*, Phaidon 1952/80

Marion Woodman: *The Pregnant Virgin: A Process of Psychological Transformation*, Inner City Books, Toronto 1989

Manfred Wudram: *Art of the Renaissance*, Weidenfeld & Nicolson 1985

J.E. Zeigler: "The Medieval Virgin as Object: Art of Anthropology?", *Historical Reflections*, XVI, 1989

Charles Zika: "Hosts, Processions and Pilgrimages: Controlling the Sacred in Fifteenth-Century Germany", *Past and Present*, CXVIII, 1988

CRESCENT MOON PUBLISHING

web: www.crmoon.com e-mail: cresmopub@yahoo.co.uk

ARTS, PAINTING, SCULPTURE

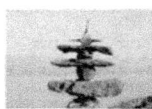
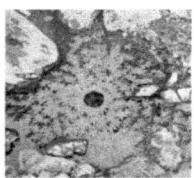
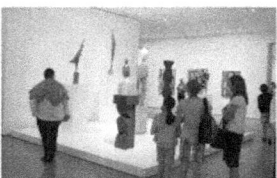
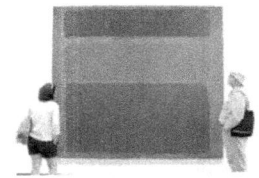

The Art of Andy Goldsworthy
Andy Goldsworthy: Touching Nature
Andy Goldsworthy in Close-Up
Andy Goldsworthy: Pocket Guide
Andy Goldsworthy In America
Land Art: A Complete Guide
The Art of Richard Long
Richard Long: Pocket Guide
Land Art In the UK
Land Art in Close-Up
Land Art In the U.S.A.
Land Art: Pocket Guide
Installation Art in Close-Up
Minimal Art and Artists In the 1960s and After
Colourfield Painting
Land Art DVD, TV documentary
Andy Goldsworthy DVD, TV documentary

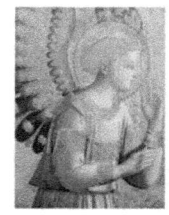

The Erotic Object: Sexuality in Sculpture From Prehistory to the Present Day
Sex in Art: Pornography and Pleasure in Painting and Sculpture
Postwar Art
Sacred Gardens: The Garden in Myth, Religion and Art
Glorification: Religious Abstraction in Renaissance and 20th Century Art
Early Netherlandish Painting
Leonardo da Vinci
Piero della Francesca
Giovanni Bellini

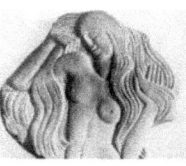
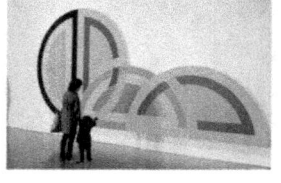

Fra Angelico: Art and Religion in the Renaissance
Mark Rothko: The Art of Transcendence
Frank Stella: American Abstract Artist
Jasper Johns
Brice Marden
Alison Wilding: The Embrace of Sculpture

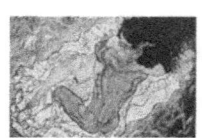
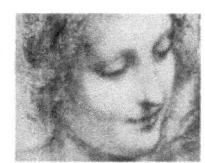

Vincent van Gogh: Visionary Landscapes
Eric Gill: Nuptials of God
Constantin Brancusi: Sculpting the Essence of Things
Max Beckmann
Caravaggio
Gustave Moreau
Egon Schiele: Sex and Death In Purple Stockings
Delizioso Fotografico Fervore: Works In Process 1
Sacro Cuore: Works In Process 2
The Light Eternal: J.M.W. Turner
The Madonna Glorified: Karen Arthurs

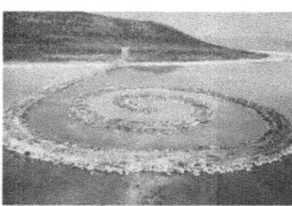

LITERATURE

J.R.R. Tolkien: The Books, The Films, The Whole Cultural Phenomenon
J.R.R. Tolkien: Pocket Guide
Tolkien's Heroic Quest
The *Earthsea* Books of Ursula Le Guin
Beauties, Beasts and Enchantment: Classic French Fairy Tales
German Popular Stories by the Brothers Grimm
Philip Pullman and *His Dark Materials*
Sexing Hardy: Thomas Hardy and Feminism
Thomas Hardy's *Tess of the d'Urbervilles*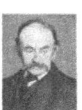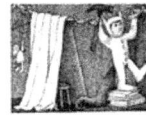
Thomas Hardy's *Jude the Obscure*
Thomas Hardy: The Tragic Novels
Love and Tragedy: Thomas Hardy
The Poetry of Landscape in Hardy
Wessex Revisited: Thomas Hardy and John Cowper Powys
Wolfgang Iser: Essays and Interviews
Petrarch, Dante and the Troubadours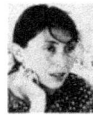
Maurice Sendak and the Art of Children's Book Illustration
Andrea Dworkin
Cixous, Irigaray, Kristeva: The *Jouissance* of French Feminism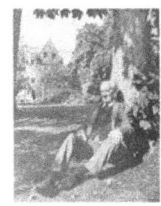
Julia Kristeva: Art, Love, Melancholy, Philosophy, Semiotics and Psychoanalysis
Hélène Cixous I Love You: The *Jouissance* of Writing
Luce Irigaray: Lips, Kissing, and the Politics of Sexual Difference
Peter Redgrove: Here Comes the Flood
Peter Redgrove: Sex-Magic-Poetry-Cornwall
Lawrence Durrell: Between Love and Death, East and West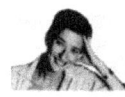
Love, Culture & Poetry: Lawrence Durrell
Cavafy: Anatomy of a Soul
German Romantic Poetry: Goethe, Novalis, Heine, Hölderlin
Feminism and Shakespeare
Shakespeare: Love, Poetry & Magic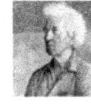
The Passion of D.H. Lawrence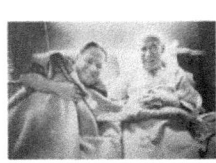
D.H. Lawrence: Symbolic Landscapes
D.H. Lawrence: Infinite Sensual Violence
Rimbaud: Arthur Rimbaud and the Magic of Poetry
The Ecstasies of John Cowper Powys
Sensualism and Mythology: The Wessex Novels of John Cowper Powys
Amorous Life: John Cowper Powys and the Manifestation of Affectivity (H.W. Fawkner)
Postmodern Powys: New Essays on John Cowper Powys (Joe Boulter)
Rethinking Powys: Critical Essays on John Cowper Powys
Paul Bowles & Bernardo Bertolucci
Rainer Maria Rilke
Joseph Conrad: *Heart of Darkness*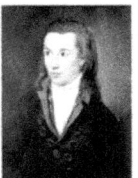
In the Dim Void: Samuel Beckett
Samuel Beckett Goes into the Silence
André Gide: Fiction and Fervour
Jackie Collins and the Blockbuster Novel
Blinded By Her Light: The Love-Poetry of Robert Graves
The Passion of Colours: Travels In Mediterranean Lands
Poetic Forms

POETRY

Ursula Le Guin: Walking In Cornwall
Peter Redgrove: Here Comes The Flood
Peter Redgrove: Sex-Magic-Poetry-Cornwall
Dante: Selections From the Vita Nuova
Petrarch, Dante and the Troubadours
William Shakespeare: Sonnets
William Shakespeare: Complete Poems
Blinded By Her Light: The Love-Poetry of Robert Graves
Emily Dickinson: Selected Poems
Emily Brontë: Poems
Thomas Hardy: Selected Poems
Percy Bysshe Shelley: Poems
John Keats: Selected Poems
Joh n Keats: Poems of 1820
D.H. Lawrence: Selected Poems
Edmund Spenser: Poems
Edmund Spenser: Amoretti
John Donne: Poems
Henry Vaughan: Poems
Sir Thomas Wyatt: Poems
Robert Herrick: Selected Poems
Rilke: Space, Essence and Angels in the Poetry of Rainer Maria Rilke
Rainer Maria Rilke: Selected Poems
Friedrich Hölderlin: Selected Poems
Arseny Tarkovsky: Selected Poems
Arthur Rimbaud: Selected Poems
Arthur Rimbaud: A Season in Hell
Arthur Rimbaud and the Magic of Poetry
Novalis: Hymns To the Night
German Romantic Poetry
Paul Verlaine: Selected Poems
Elizaethan Sonnet Cycles
D.J. Enright: By-Blows
Jeremy Reed: Brigitte's Blue Heart
Jeremy Reed: Claudia Schiffer's Red Shoes
Gorgeous Little Orpheus
Radiance: New Poems
Crescent Moon Book of Nature Poetry
Crescent Moon Book of Love Poetry
Crescent Moon Book of Mystical Poetry
Crescent Moon Book of Elizabethan Love Poetry
Crescent Moon Book of Metaphysical Poetry
Crescent Moon Book of Romantic Poetry
Pagan America: New American Poetry

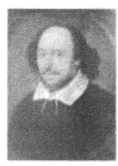
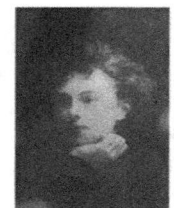
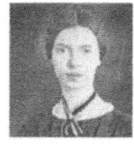
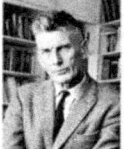

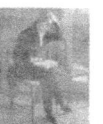
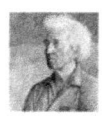
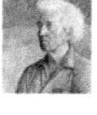
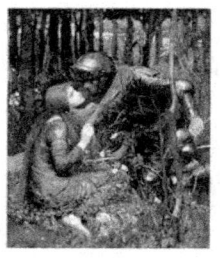
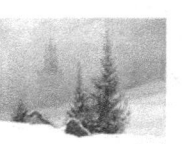
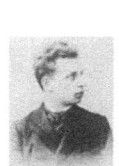
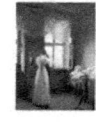
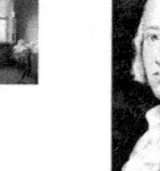
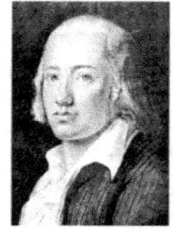

MEDIA, CINEMA, FEMINISM and CULTURAL STUDIES

J.R.R. Tolkien: The Books, The Films, The Whole Cultural Phenomenon
J.R.R. Tolkien: Pocket Guide
The *Lord of the Rings* Movies: Pocket Guide
The Cinema of Hayao Miyazaki
Hayao Miyazaki: *Princess Mononoke*: Pocket Movie Guide
Hayao Miyazaki: *Spirited Away*: Pocket Movie Guide
Tim Burton : Hallowe'en For Hollywood
Ken Russell
Ken Russell: *Tommy*: Pocket Movie Guide

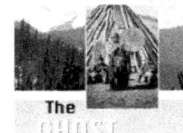
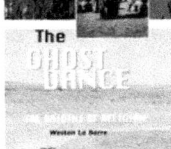

The Ghost Dance: The Origins of Religion
The Peyote Cult
Cixous, Irigaray, Kristeva: The *Jouissance* of French Feminism
Julia Kristeva: Art, Love, Melancholy, Philosophy, Semiotics and Psychoanalysis
Luce Irigaray: Lips, Kissing, and the Politics of Sexual Difference
Hélène Cixous I Love You: The *Jouissance* of Writing
Andrea Dworkin
'Cosmo Woman': The World of Women's Magazines
Women in Pop Music
HomeGround: The Kate Bush Anthology
Discovering the Goddess (Geoffrey Ashe)

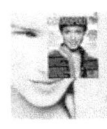
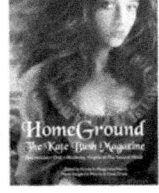

The Poetry of Cinema
The Sacred Cinema of Andrei Tarkovsky
Andrei Tarkovsky: Pocket Guide
Andrei Tarkovsky: *Mirror*: Pocket Movie Guide
Andrei Tarkovsky: *The Sacrifice*: Pocket Movie Guide
Walerian Borowczyk: Cinema of Erotic Dreams
Jean-Luc Godard: The Passion of Cinema
Jean-Luc Godard: *Hail Mary*: Pocket Movie Guide
Jean-Luc Godard: *Contempt*: Pocket Movie Guide

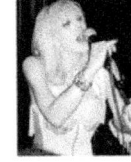

Jean-Luc Godard: *Pierrot le Fou*: Pocket Movie Guide
John Hughes and Eighties Cinema
Ferris Bueller's Day Off: Pocket Movie Guide
Jean-Luc Godard: Pocket Guide

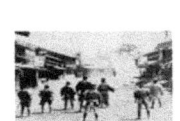
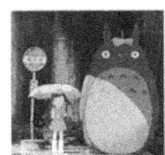

The Cinema of Richard Linklater
Liv Tyler: Star In Ascendance
Blade Runner and the Films of Philip K. Dick
Paul Bowles and Bernardo Bertolucci
Media Hell: Radio, TV and the Press
An Open Letter to the BBC

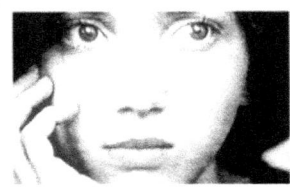

Detonation Britain: Nuclear War in the UK
Feminism and Shakespeare
Wild Zones: Pornography, Art and Feminism
Sex in Art: Pornography and Pleasure in Painting and Sculpture
Sexing Hardy: Thomas Hardy and Feminism

The Light Eternal is a model monograph, an exemplary job. The subject matter of the book is beautifully organised and dead on beam. (Lawrence Durrell)
It is amazing for me to see my work treated with such passion and respect. (Andrea Dworkin)

CRESCENT MOON PUBLISHING
P.O. Box 1312, Maidstone, Kent, ME14 5XU, Great Britain. www.crmoon.com

cresmopub@yahoo.co.uk   www.crescentmoon.org.uk